AND THEN I CRIED:

Stories of a Mortuary NCO

Justin Jordan

TACTI6AL

Published by Tactical 16, LLC
Colorado Springs, CO

eISBN: 978-0-9855582-2-2
ISBN: 978-0-9855582-5-3 (hc)
ISBN: 978-0-9855582-4-6 (sc)

Printed in the United States of America

Dedicated to SPC David W. Taylor, a hometown hero who sacrificed his life in the defense of our freedom, and to the true heroes in my life, my family: Shar Jordan, Dimitrius Williams Jr. and Summer Jordan.

- Justin Jordan

SPECIAL THANKS

How do you thank someone you have never met that has supported you without ever even laying eyes on your direction? These people are a special kind of awesome, they give of themselves without hesitation or provocation. These are my heroes, they give me strength to carry on every day, knowing my journey is worthwhile, no matter how cumbersome it sometimes may seem. They have inspired me to keep my head up, chest out and to walk again with pride. I will admit I have days that I just want to stick my head in the sand so none of the bad things can get me, but then I remember these people who believed in me, my work, and my future. So I pull myself together and move past the hurt, to a place of healing and advocacy for those who aren't as strong and have no voice. I hesitated naming these people here at first, because not one of them supported me for anything other than just that, a helping hand when a guy needed it. These are the people that are helping me get my story to the masses in print form. After a lot of thought I have reconsidered the notion and now find it very appropriate to name them here. These amazing men and women are **Mr. James Cox, Dr. Debbie Chapman, Mr. Chad Gregory, Mr. Herb H. Hennell** and **Mr. Ed Shahzade**. These fine people have given me more than words can express and I will forever be grateful for your generosity.

CONTENTS

FOREWARD

I looked up, my head pounding, the radio tuned to my favorite talk radio show. Everything seemed hazy and for a moment I thought I had just been in a car wreck. I was stricken with panic. *"Oh My God, what happened? Where am I? Am I hurt? Is anyone else hurt?"* My panic was heightened and the sound of a car horn blasted through my reality. As the long tunnel closed and my vision cleared, I came back to the reality of my surroundings. I realize I'm sitting at a stoplight on a street I don't recognize. I hit the gas and pull into a fast food restaurant parking lot and slam my truck into park. As I try to catch my breath, I start looking around for signs or landmarks that may give me some clue to my whereabouts. As hard as I try, I cannot make out anything that is familiar to me. As panic tightened its grip on my mind I reached for my phone. I enabled the GPS and the round circle started spinning looking for my location. A blue dot popped up on the map just north of Santa Fe, New Mexico. *"What, Santa Fe. Holy Shit, how did I get here?"* I thought to myself. The panic turned to real concern and fear. I lived nearly 120 miles from the location I was currently at. My last conscious thought I can remember is I had been leaving the base on my way home for the day in Albuquerque. This was not the first time this had happened to me. A year before it had happened while living in Arizona. At the time I chalked it up to being overtired and overworked, but this time was different. I remember being almost run over in the parking lot, which stirred up a lot of anxiety in me as I had seen a friend killed in a parking lot. So needless to say parking lots have never been my favorite place. To lose that much time was a problem. I immediately started thinking the worst. *"It's a brain tumor or a stroke, maybe I was abducted by aliens, and after all I am in New Mexico."* I chuckled to myself as I always enjoyed making people laugh even if it was me. All kidding aside, I had a problem, a real living breathing issue. I decided to start on the trek home so I looked down at my phone and started to follow the blue line illuminated on my phone screen. The problem with such a long drive home is that I had a lot of time to think, to dwell, to worry.

Just months prior I had been diagnosed with Post Traumatic Stress Disorder

(PTSD) and had been moved to a special duty assignment outside my normal career field in hopes of alleviating my symptoms that were becoming unmanageable at my current duty station. I had thought I had fixed the problem and I had been cured. I was oblivious that this incident may have been a symptom of PTSD. On that journey home I decided to ignore what I now know was a disassociation. My thought process told me that if I ignored the problem it would go away, and besides I was cured. At my previous base in Arizona and on several deployments I was a Mortuary NCO, the grim reaper if you will. In the six years prior I had seen more death and bodies than any human should ever see. I had seen murders, suicides, drownings, war dead, and even strokes. I had stared into the eyes of my own mortality and didn't blink on more than one occasion. It took a huge toll on my mental well-being and now I'm paying the price in spades. I decided to suppress my feelings. My new co-workers and bosses would not understand, my wife and my kids wouldn't understand, fuck, I didn't understand. We are taught as young men on the football fields and baseball diamonds of America, "Suck it up, quit being a baby, and leave it on the field." Now as a grown man with a family of his own, I'm scared, no, not scared, terrified and not just sometimes, all the time. Why can't I just suck it up, or leave it on the field. What is wrong with me?

During my recovery I have suffered from debilitating fear, hyper vigilance, avoidance, dissociative attacks, and olfactory hallucinations. I have been in therapy for the better part of three years and have spent 30 days in an inpatient treatment center all in an effort to beat PTSD. I maintain to this day, I WILL NOT LET THIS BEAT ME. I take you now on a journey, a walk in my shoes if you will. I hold back nothing; I pull back the curtain on death and show you the inevitable fate we will all succumb to someday. I did not write this to shock you, or to get your sympathy, but to educate you. Hopefully you will gain a small bit of insight on the affliction that hundreds of thousands of our veterans suffer from in silence. I invite you now to take a walk with me and carry my pain, even if for just a little while.

INTRODUCTION

"As I walk through the valley of the shadow of death, I will fear no evil..." Well, I think that is bullshit! I am scared of everything. I have seen behind the proverbial curtain and what I have seen does not make me feel safe, ever. I struggle with life as I have seen, felt, tasted, and heard death, over and over, repeated day in and day out. I am not the type of person that gives up or lets things overwhelm me. For the first time in my life I have challenged something that is a worthy adversary.

In this book you will find stories of some of my experiences as a Mortuary Affairs NCOIC (Non Commissioned Officer in Charge.) There are many more that I just couldn't add. I will share them with you the way I remember them in all their graphic detail. I will also share with you how I felt at that particular moment in time. I sometimes worry that my mind has filled in blanks in my memory and it is my sincerest hope that this is not true. But I had to write down what I have seen and how I remember it. All of the chapters except one are an exact retelling of my experiences; this one chapter is a recount one of my reoccurring dreams. I added this to illustrate just how vivid the memories can be, even if they are generated in the mind. This is a big step in my battle with PTSD and by sharing these horrible things it takes some of the burden off of me. It has taken a long time to accept that it is ok to share my pain; I can carry it no more. If while reading this you are touched by my stories, I say to you, *"Thank you. Thank you for carrying some of that pain."* I have changed the names of the deceased to protect their families and loved ones' privacy and dignity. But know this, I remember every syllable of their names and it is not meant to be disrespectful. I have worked more deaths than I can remember. However, the ones detailed in this book are the ones that had a profound impact on my mental well-being. I blame no one. I am not bitter. I am glad I had these experiences because they have challenged me to overcome my adversity, and made my life extraordinary. If at any time while reading this book a tear falls from your cheek, I ask of you one favor, let it hit the page, in remembrance of the fallen brave men and women who gave of themselves to protect and defend your freedom.

The Plight of a Man

THE PLIGHT

Do you understand, the plight of a man, the plight of a man,
do you really understand?
I walk alone scared, afraid to share, afraid to feel, what is normal, what is real?
My kids, my family, I leave them behind; they all think I have lost my mind.
They care, they try, but who wants to see their father cry?
I'm supposed to be the rock, the tower, the ultimate power,
but instead they get to see me cower.
I've let them down, how could I let my family drown?
I try, I try, to see the bright side, the light side, but I can't seem to let it slide
The nameless faces, the god-awful places, the voided spaces in my mind,
I can't leave them behind.
I sit amongst strangers, reliving dangers, hoping to grab just a little relief,
even if it may be brief.
My dreams are endless and replay all day, I hide the fear,
I mean what should I say?
Should I say I'm scared, I'm nervous, I'm losing my mind?
What would they do with information of that kind?
Would they tell me its ok, or it will be all right, will that help me get
through the night?
I want so badly to be normal again, to live life without the dreams within.
I grasp for help anywhere I can, but will they ever, can they ever,
understand the plight of this man?

"Suffer in Silence" © 2012 Gaz Mather, www.uecriticalmass.co.uk

CHAPTER 1
We Do WHAT?

It was the summer of 1993. I had just finished Basic Military Training at Lackland AFB in San Antonio, Texas. I arrived at my Technical Training School at Lowery AFB, Colorado, a beautiful base nestled at the base of the Rocky Mountains. I joined the United States Air Force after I tried my hand at college and a short stint as a factory worker. After high school, I was bored and wanted to get out and see the world. Small town life was not for me. As the son of two dedicated educators, my view of the world was one of endless possibilities, and none of them involved me staying in Henderson, Kentucky. After job certification and classification I was informed that I would be in the Morale Welfare Recreation and Services career field. This interested me because I was an athlete in high school, and had a fondness for sports. We were told that we would be working in the Fitness and Recreation Centers, doing things like intramural sports programming and recreational events planning. To say I was excited was an understatement. Little did I know that my world, my perception, my path was about to change. At the time, the military did not represent anything but a job, which had great benefits. I was, however, a patriotic person, so that also appealed to me. The thought of dying in the line of duty never crossed my mind. In retrospect, that is a very naive view of the world. But I was happy being ignorant, extremely happy. The first day of class the Military Training Leaders huddle all of the new Airmen in a classroom. They told us that the first order of business would be to report to the warehouse to be fitted for our cook whites. My mind paused, I thought to myself, *"Cook's whites? What do you mean? Oh...I must be in the wrong class, because I am going to be a sports and recreation guy."* I raised my hand in hopes of finding my way to the correct classroom, because, let's face it; I am nobody's cook. I asked the instructors where I should go as I was in the wrong class. The instructors all chuckled simultaneously and then there was silence. My question had piqued curiosity in all of the students. The senior instructor broke the silence with his arrogant tone, "What, they didn't tell you? Our career field has merged with the Services career field and now you all will be cooks. If you're lucky in about ten years you may be able to work in the fitness center." A clap of laughter ignited among the instructors, and at the same time disappointment fell over the faces of every Airman in the room. I soon found out every one of us felt as though we had been wrongly assigned. I forgot everything I had been taught in the previous six weeks of basic military training, the countless lessons on never questioning superiors, the constant barking of orders 24 hours a day, in an attempt to transform us from civilians to Airmen. That's it! Where is my Congressman? I have been wronged! No, lied to! I was not told I would be a cook. I am nobody's cook! The anger, disappointment, and sheer fear of being seen as less than spectacular in my family and circle of friends seemed unbearable to me.

After several days of sulking and many calls home, I eventually swallowed that disappointment and pressed on with training. Many of the Non Commissioned Officer (NCO) instructors had tried to alleviate our anxiety, they told us we would be more employable when we left the military, or that we did not have to turn the same wrench for twenty years, like the mechanics. They told us we could do different jobs, and that cooking was just one of them. I wasn't buying it; I felt they were patronizing me. I would sit in the dormitory at night and voice my concerns to other trainees. It seemed like I gained some type of strength from being in the group. It was my only relief and none of us felt we had a voice. I spent all day in training just yearning for the night, so I could sit with my friends and bitch. As training progressed I learned that the career field to which I had been assigned was considered the Air Forces' "jack of all trades." We did everything from cook to hotel and club management, fitness and recreation, and in some locations we would be trained to tend bar. There was one job that took me by surprise and left me puzzled. It seems we also handled Mortuary Affairs for the Air Force. *"What?!" Why on earth would the cooks handle the dead?"* Years later, a boss of mine told me it was because we owned all of the refrigerators on base, but that was purely his opinion and to date I haven't heard a better explanation. I went through the technical training with very little training in any of the other areas of my career field. We focused solely on food preparation and our deployment mission which seemed a little like chuck wagon cooking. Six weeks later, I graduated from training and was assigned to my first base Ramstein AB,

Germany.

After arriving in Germany, I spent most of my time in the flight feeding facility cooking for pilots, Security Forces (Cops) that guarded the planes and the maintainers who fixed the planes. One day I asked my supervisor, a red headed lanky Staff Sergeant who spent more time at the racquetball courts than he did at the job, about the mortuary aspect of our job. His eyes became cold and dark; his tone was somber and grim. "Son, you don't want to know, no seriously, you don't want to know. It will be better if you focus on your current job. You will have plenty of time to learn the dark side of our business." I gave him a puzzled look and dismissed myself. Being the curious sort, I started asking some of my peers what they had heard and none of them, not one, understood exactly what it was we did. Scratching my head with frustration, I finally decided to stop by my Chief Master Sergeant's office to ask him. The Chief was a wise looking, older, black gentleman whose face was withered with years of service. His hair was sparse and grey. I had been told he was the answer man and I had already climbed to the proverbial top of the mountain to seek his enlightenment, so I thought to myself, *"here goes nothing."* I knocked on the door and I remember being very nervous, why, I had no idea, but I just was. I heard a gravelly voice come from within the office "Yes, may I help you?" I stepped into his office and he swung around in his chair, so I began, *"Chief, I'm Airman Jordan and I was wondering if you had a moment?"* I said in a shaky voice. The Chief replied with "I know who the hell you are, what kind of Chief would I be if I didn't know my troops? So, what can I do for you Airman?" He barked in a seemingly disapproving fashion. I responded, *"Well Chief, I have been asking everyone and no one can tell me about the mortuary aspect of our job, and I was wondering if you could fill me in?"* The Chief's brow furrowed and he asked, "Why do you want to know?" I responded with the response that I had practiced in the mirror many times, *"Chief, if I am to be the best Airman I can be, then I feel it is imperative for me to know and succeed at all aspects of my assigned duties."* I was quite proud of myself, as I had, in my mind, nailed it. The Chief looked at me with a disappointed, father-like stare, cutting me to my core and he said, "You do realize that people have to DIE in order for YOU to SUCCEED" using his fingers to make quotation marks in a condescending manor. Bewildered, I came right back at him with, *"Chief, I wish death on no one, but, wouldn't it be better if I am prepared for the worst?"* The Chief responded with "You know, Airman, you have a point." Over the next hours the Chief explained to me in great detail the many facets of the Mortuary Services and how we operate within that world. I was humbled, I left his office almost wishing I was still ignorant, but like the Chief told me just before I left his office, "You asked." The things the Chief shared with me that day weighed heavy on me for quite some time, but I had a while before I would ever have to worry about that portion of the job. Typically the mortuary was reserved for Non Commissioned Officers who had proven their abilities and could deal with the stress levels associated with those types of duties.

What the Chief shared with me that day was unbelievable to me. He told me that when a Service Member dies on Active Duty we took care of his or her remains, assuring that the utmost respect was given to the fallen. We did not handle the actual embalming, but we provided instructions to the morticians and made sure they were following appropriate protocol. We ensured they adhered to strict contract guidelines as well as making certain no illegal organ harvest had taken place. All military members who die while serving on active duty get an autopsy, typically provided by the local medical examiner. After that we meet with the family and provide them with options, such as traditional burial, cremation, dress and travel arrangements. This is at no cost to the family, within a budgetary cap, which is significantly ample to pay for the funeral expenses. We would then meet with the Funeral Director at the funeral home of the families' choosing and view the remains. More often than not the families choose to use our contracted funeral home; it was a much easier process for them because they typically were from out of town. We would go through a series of steps during these inspections, almost always post autopsy. During the first inspection the remains are not sewn up and there are large gaping holes in the chest where the organs were removed and weighed. The skull had been removed at the crown horizontally, and on rare occasions the incision was from ear to ear vertically. This was done to remove the brain for the purpose of toxicology, and possible disease findings. We provided the Funeral Director instructions on disposition of the remains on the family's behalf. Instructions often included such things as tissue build up, laceration closing, makeup application, and dressing the remains in the uniform. This was done in an attempt to leave the family with the best possible last memory. We then leave the professionals to do their job and make an appointment to review the remains after the embalming process is complete. At this inspection we ensure the embalming is sufficiently completed, by feeling different parts of the remains to ensure proper rigidity. We also turn the remains on its side to ensure that no hypodermic embalming needed to be accomplished. To further explain this step, the body will pool blood and fluids in the back postmortem, typical embalming does not always account for this, so to prevent leakage we may have to instruct the mortician to hypodermically embalm those areas, especially if the remains will be traveling to another location. Once we agree that the embalming has been successful, we make another appointment to view the makeup application and the uniform fitting to ensure the remains are dressed correctly, and they present a proper military image. This whole time we have been meeting with the NOK (Next of Kin) to ensure their wishes are strictly followed, and to arrange travel and a Military Escort of the remains to the final resting place, which is chosen by the family. We also arrange an Honor Guard at the location of burial, and if authorized we coordinate fly overs for aviators. That sounds like a lot to do, but that's only half of the mission. As the Chief explained further to me, we also do search and recovery. This is a team of individuals that go onto locations where aircraft have crashed and remove the human remains. It may be fingers and toes, eyeballs, or whole souls, as we call them. It's an arduous process that could take weeks, depending on the terrain, soil type, and weather. He went even further and explained our wartime mission which had been coined as the "bag tag and ship process." We would collect remains from the battlefield casualty collection point and gather any personal effects, place them in a body bag, put identification tags on the remains, ice the remains and place them in a transfer case for air shipment to Dover Air Force Base, where the Port Mortuary is located. I was floored by the sheer importance of the task, but it left me puzzled again. I thought to myself, *"Why us? What sense did it* ____ *the medics be doing this?"* It has been over 19 years now ____ given me a valid response to that quest___ ____ Sergeant. Sometimes I reflect back to ____ ignorance, and how my opinions on life and now death were very, very naive.

CHAPTER 2
To War and to Texas Sprinkled With a Little More War

I spent the next two years in Germany cooking for the base populace and working in the in-flight feed facility. This was exciting to me because our kitchen was at the end of the flight line; I would get to see each plane take off and land. The base had a very busy mission with a lot of fighter planes and some C-5 cargo planes; these are behemoth planes the size of a football field. I became very close to my friends on the base and we traveled extensively throughout Europe. I felt like a big deal because I made it out of my small hometown and I was going to Paris, Amsterdam, and Berlin. I did not look forward to my time ending in Germany, but it was inevitable, as a first tour overseas only lasted two years. I did, however, begin to look forward to finding out where my next assignment would be and going home on leave to brag about my tour overseas.

One day, very near to the end of my tour of duty, I was called into my readiness office to meet with the deployment manager. I thought I would be briefed about my next assignment; so I hurried over there to get the good news. I arrived at the office and the NCO in charge greeted me at the door. He was in his middle thirties, a slim gentleman that appeared to take great pride in his uniform. His uniform looked as if could stand up on its own, and his boots resembled black mirrors. He asked "Are you ready?" I looked at him and said, *"Ready to PCS, yes sir?"* (PCS is permanent change of station.) He grinned and said, "No, ready to deploy." My face must have twisted in a way that seemed disrespectful to him because he got extremely angry with me and said, "Look, you're in the military, son. You swore an oath to fight and defend your country, so I'll ask you again are you ready to deploy?" Without thinking I said *"Yes, sir!"* He then began to brief me on my mission to Khobar Towers in Dhahran, Saudi Arabia. He explained how I would be providing quality assurance services by monitoring the contract cooks that were feeding the troops deployed there. The next thing I remember, I was on a plane to the Middle East. The flight sucked; as I was in the air for seemingly days and my feet were swollen up to nearly double their size from the change in air pressure. I could literally feel my heart beating in the soles of my feet. On the bright side, I did get issued the new desert colored uniforms, which I thought were pretty nice, and a lot lighter in weight than the battle dress uniform I was accustomed to wearing. We touched down in Saudi Arabia and I remember thinking, *"What the fuck is this?"* Everything was dirty and dusty, and it was as hot outside as I had ever experienced. It was almost like I had opened an oven on my face, and someone was spraying me with sand. I arrived at Khobar Towers to find that we were staying in these extravagant towering apartment complexes with marble floors and cable T.V., I thought to myself, *"If this was what war was like, count me in."* I was assigned to work in the "chow hall", a term cooks find offensive, but I always kind of liked it. We watched the TCNs (third country nationals) who cooked our food, making sure they did not go outside the compound or do anything to the food that may cause the base population to fall ill. We also ensured they adhered to the nutritional guidelines set by the Air Force, basically, mind numbing work. I soon found out, being deployed was a big party. We went downtown to the gold malls to shop, and since there was no alcohol allowed in Saudi Arabia, we were forced to travel to Bahrain every weekend to drink at the Naval Air Station. In my time there I developed close relationships with the TCNs that I worked alongside of. They were genuine people that were paid slave wages; they were by far the hardest working group of people I had ever had the pleasure of working with. We were all feeling very privileged and had a sense of safety and security, that in looking back, I can't fathom how we were so clueless to the threats. My time in the desert flew by; I made friends that I still speak with to this day. I never considered that anyone would want to hurt us, or target us; it just never entered my mind. I arrived back home 90 days later and was immediately told that I was to be stationed at Lackland AFB, in San Antonio, Texas. This information troubled me, because I had been there for basic training and had very bad memories of that place. I was told it was *"The needs of the Air Force"*, a phrase I would hear a million times over in my nearly 20 year career.

I arrived in Texas and was assigned to one of the Basic Military Training Squadrons to oversee the new recruits doing kitchen detail. Basically, I yelled at Airmen to clean dishes harder and faster. I was such a hypocrite, I hated how I was treated in basic, but the first opportunity I got to put that same pain on others, I jumped on it. I was only there a few months before I received another deployment order to return back to the base in Saudi Arabia, it had been on the news a lot. They had just been hit by a massive truck bomb crumbling several of the villas, very close to the one I stayed in. This is the first time I can ever remember being afraid for my life. But, once again, the needs of the Air Force outweighed my measly concerns. I do remember distinctly hearing my old deployment manager in my thoughts, "You signed up to defend your country, son" and at that moment I was never happier, to be just a cook.

I arrived back in Saudi Arabia to find a much different existence. We were on Prince Sultan Air Base, a base in the middle of nowhere. It literally was the closest thing to hell I could imagine. The base was nothing but tents and a flight line. There were no toilets or showers, just tents, when we finally did get toilets and showers they were setup in tents that lacked in the area of privacy. I can remember taking a shit and a guy would be rubbing elbows with me while he shaved with bottled water. We were not allowed to leave the base and our mission was very clear, enforce the no fly zone in Iraq. There were nearly eight thousand coalition forces there and we had to feed them all. I had a pretty cool job; I was in charge of transferring the food that was flown in on aircraft, to the food warehouse, which was a collection of 20 refrigerated trailers, much like you would see behind any big rig on American highways. One day that sticks out in my mind on this deployment, is the day my front-end loader broke, I was stuck out in the desert, away from everything, with no help in sight. Eventually after seeing no one in a while, I decided to walk to base. I quickly figured out why the traffic stopped during that time. The area was blanketed with a huge sand storm and as I got closer to base the storm hit me. It was like being shot with a thousand small pieces of lead, with unrelenting force. Although I kept my head down as I walked, the sand filled my eyes, and it caked onto my tear ducts. As I breathed, I took sand into my lungs, causing me to cough so violently I vomited. The whole time I thought to myself, *"You can't stop."* I had to make it to the shelter of the base, and I had already traveled past the point where it would have been farther to walk back to the loader and wait it out. I was stuck and as the fear mounted, I truly thought I was going to die that day, in the sand, far from home, all alone. I eventually made it to base and ducked into the guard shack with the cops that were also huddled inside trying to weather the storm. They gave me water and patched me up and we all sat there in silence and experienced each other's fear. Not a word was spoken, but a ton was being said. We all missed home, we were all scared, and not one of us had ever experienced something so violent.

After the storm blew over, I went back to my tent and fell into my cot like a sack of bricks. I fell asleep almost instantly. The next morning I awoke coughing worse than I had ever coughed before. It was unbearable; I could hardly catch a breath between coughs. I was burning up but I wasn't sweating, and I felt dizzy. I looked and sounded so dismal my tent mates rushed me to the hospital. I was seen immediately and they admitted me for a bad case of bronchitis and severe dehydration. The medics tried for hours to start an IV line on me to help with the dehydration but no one could get a line in my veins. I was also on a steady stream of oxygen. As I lay there, scared as shit, I overheard the doctors talking about medevac'ing me to Germany as my condition grew more dire. I remember thinking to myself, *"No! I made it through the mother fucking storm! I'm not going to die in a tent surrounded by incompetent medics, who can't even start a fucking IV!"* Just then, a young Airman medic approached me and said, "Hey man, so what happened to you?" I tried to tell him but speaking just brought on a coughing fit. He looked at me and said, "Oh, you must have gotten caught out in that sand storm. You probably sucked in a lot of sand." I nodded and he said, "Well let's get you fixed up." His confidence was strangely comforting, and on his first try he was able to find a vein and the IV fluids started flowing. I instantly started to feel better and after three long days in the hospital I returned to work, a lucky young man. I spent the rest of my tour there working my ass off, sometimes for 16 hour days, delivering food, helping out in the kitchen when necessary and pulling the occasional stranded vehicle out of the sand with my front-end loader. I was now a war hardened killing... umm, scratch that, a war hardened cooking machine.

I returned to Lackland and settled back into my role as kitchen dictator, but I wanted so badly to work in the fitness center. Every week for months on end I would stop by my boss' office and ask for a transfer into the fitness area of our career field. He told me the same thing every time "Airman Jordan, you will go where you're needed. Right now we need you to work in the training squadron." I was relentless and week after week I bugged him until one day he snapped, "Ok you persistent fucking asshole, go see the fitness director, and ask if he is willing to trade someone for you. FUCK! Now, get the hell out of here!" I left there with a grin from ear to ear; I had a knack for getting my way. It was late in the day on a Friday so I knew my meeting with the Sports and Fitness Director would have to wait until Monday, but I did not care, because change, it was a coming. Monday morning I met with him and sure enough I talked my way into a job. For the next several years I ran a small fitness center on the far side of base. It was very interesting to me, but what was really important to me was, I never had to tell people I was a cook again, well, at least not at this base. This is where my career really took off; I enjoyed what I did and excelled at it. My new position brought many accolades from my leadership; I won several annual awards for excellence. This is also about the time I met the woman I would spend the rest of my life with, my wife Shar.

I attended a party my friend had taken me to. It was a house party with only a few people there, more like a BBQ than a house party. I grew bored of the idle chitchat in the garage and decided to go check out the back yard. When I got there I saw this tiny little kid, who couldn't have been more than two years old. He was trying his damnedest to throw this football that was almost as big as he was. I chuckled at the site of him and approached him and said, *"Hey little man, you need some help?"* He looked at me and frowned and pulled the ball away from me as if to say "MY BALL." I said, *"Ok, ok."* I motioned for him to toss it to me, he obliged, and that started an hour long pitch and catch session that neither of us ever seemed to tire of. Over my shoulder I noticed a woman standing at the door. Our eyes met and she smiled and said, "Dimitrius, are you having fun?" He nodded his head with a resounding yes. She came out and watched us play for a while; we had met earlier in the front yard. She told me her name was Shar Williams and that she was recently married. I got the feeling by the way she described her husband that she wasn't happy. The child I was playing football with was her son, Dimitrius Williams Jr., a two-and-a-half year old African American child with thick curly brown hair and big brown eyes that would melt your heart on sight. Since Shar was Caucasian I assumed that meant her husband was African American. Over the next few months Shar seemed to be at every party I was at. She made her interest in me very clear, but I was raised not to

11

mess with married women. So I avoided her, it got so bad that at one point I told her point blank, *"When you get a divorce, call me. Until then, leave me the fuck alone!"* Don't get me wrong, I was flattered, but I just couldn't mess around with another man's woman.

A couple of months later I received a call from Shar. She was divorced and needed a place to stay. Since we had an extra bedroom in the house we were renting, it made perfect sense. She moved in that day and except for deployments we haven't spent a day apart since. Shar has been my rock, she too is in the Air Force and we instantly became best friends, we found comfort in each other having so much in common. As for Dimitrius, he has been a great son, I love him like he's my blood. He's almost 18 now and I am so proud of the man he has become. Even though we have had some bumps along the way, he has proven to be a kind, thoughtful man who I admire. We also have a daughter together, Summer Jordan, who is the most wonderful, tender hearted girl you could ever meet. She's nearly 13 and has become quite a creative and smart young woman. Every day she gives me another reason to be proud of her, and to top it all off, she's pretty funny too. Shar was a military brat who lived overseas in Germany until her senior year in high school. Since then she has been living in San Antonio, Texas where her father retired from the Air Force. She had been assigned as a Health Care Administrator at Wilford Hall Medical Center. We were married after two years of living together and after spending nearly six years in Texas, the time came for a new assignment. I had applied to be a Combat Readiness Instructor at the world famous Silver Flag Combat Training Site at Tyndall AFB, FL. Not to my surprise, I was hired and off we went to set up shop in Florida. I could not wait. Florida here we come!

CHAPTER 3
Florida....Yes!

I had made it! I was Cadre at the very prestigious 823rd DET 1 Red Horse Squadron, located in Panama City Florida on Tyndall AFB. It was a large collection of sixty plus engineers and there were thirteen of us cooks. We concentrated on teaching combat feeding, lodging, fitness, recreation, force bed down operations and wartime mortuary operations. This was to be my first experience with the mortuary subject matter but it wasn't real. It was all, what if's, and hypothetical situations. We prided ourselves in realism and often used local butchers to provide animal innards to authenticate the training. Typically we would use cow brains and intestines to train wartime search and recovery operations. I had never been a part of such a tight knit unit, we were all family. We worked our asses off all day and partied together all night. Our families were close and you could always count on your fellow cadre to be there, no matter what. Looking back, I miss the camaraderie. I have never before, nor have I since, experienced such a feeling of belonging to a unit. A short time after my arrival, I met my soon to be best friend, Derek Kelly. He was and still is the cockiest son of a bitch you will ever meet. But the thing about Derek is, you want him in your foxhole, he would die before he let anything happen to one of his friends. I miss him a lot, although we still talk, our conversations have become less frequent as the years pass. Nonetheless, I will always consider him to be my brother.

A day I will never forget is the day I encountered my first real deceased service member. I had been offered the opportunity to travel to Ft Dix, New Jersey to deliver some training to another group of instructors on a new troop housing system called the Small Shelter System (SSS). Our unit had been training this module for quite some time and Ft Dix had just received their first shipment of SSS's. I was excited and nervous to be one of the trainers selected to go, as it said something about my ability to train other experts. In my experience other instructors are super critical of technique and make the worst students. They hang on every word and let you know the second you make even the slightest mistake. Nevertheless, I was looking forward to the challenge; I knew deep down I could succeed. There were three of us on this trip me, Derek, and our boss whom we referred to as Boz. Boz was a very lighthearted fellow who seemed to instantly deflate any tense situation with humor. However, he could also be very stern and serious, a signature trait of most senior Non Commissioned Officers.

We arrived and Derek and I took turns instructing each module. When we completed the instruction we were immediately giddy with cockiness, as we felt we had nailed it. Yet another feather in the cap of the 823rd RHS Cadre, these are the things decorations are made of, so needless to say, we were very proud of ourselves. We had one more day left on our trip, Boz had arranged for us tour the Port Mortuary facilities at Dover AFB. He felt it would help us gain perspective on our mortuary classes. Derek and I reluctantly agreed, It wasn't like we could tell him no, he's the boss. The next day we all piled into the rental car and drove to Delaware.

Upon our arrival, I remember thinking that the building looked like any other building adjacent to the flight line. It was a brown painted brick building that could have been mistaken for a maintenance back shop, except for the sign saying Air Force Port Mortuary. We entered and met with the head Air Force mortician, whose name escapes me. He showed us the lobby equipped with a family briefing room and the decorations room. The decorations room housed every combination of uniform ever used in service. It included all branches of service and every ribbon or decoration ever created. They went to extreme lengths to ensure any deceased service member returning home was dressed appropriately in uniform with the correct decorations on their uniform. We were led into the back of the facility to the off-loading area where a series of tables fitted with metal rollers like those you might see in a warehouse, were lined up ready to receive transfer cases housing the remains of our countries war dead. The transfer team would unload the remains from an aircraft and place them on these tables. From that point the remains are rolled down the line into a state of the art 4D scanner. The scanner is used by bomb technicians to ensure that no unexploded ordinance is lodged inside the remains. Next, the remains are sent to a station operated by the FBI where fingerprints are taken from the remains and analyzed by their database. The remains are then transferred to the dental station for dental record processing. All of this is performed in an effort to irrefutably identify the deceased. I was awe struck by the extent to which those who ran the facility went to ensure the dignified handling of each set of remains.

As we rounded the corner from the receiving area we entered into the personal effects room. This was a very large room full of tables covered with wallets, watches, wedding rings, pictures of kids, and dog tags that were being prepared for return to the families of the deceased. The sight of this room hit me hard, I watched as the technicians cleaned dried blood off of each personal effect. I remember thinking, *"that watch looks like mine."* Suddenly, the experience of standing in that room became personal. I stared down at my own watch, making comparisons, and there it was, standing in front of me, my mortality. I was facing it for the first time, I did not like the feeling, I was flushed and warm, sounds echoed and time seemed to slow down, I digested the realism, *"It could have been me."*

Photo from the collection *"Personal Effects"* © 2009 Air Force Mortuary Affairs Operations, www.mortuary.af.mil

Another thing that stands out in my mind, even now, is the memory of a wallet lying open on a table to the picture section. Inside the plastic folder was a blood smeared picture of a little blonde girl. She was approximately 4 years old, she had the prettiest blue eyes, and a smile that could light up a city block. My lip quivered as I stood there thinking to myself, *"Her Daddy is never coming home. Who will cheer her successes? Who will kiss her head goodnight? Who will scare away the monsters when she is frightened? Who?"* It really bothered me as I thought of my own little girl and how important she was to me. I swallowed hard and felt certain that my discomfort had been noticed by the technicians. Our guide wisely sensed this and hustled us to the next room, the autopsy room. This is where the remains were taken apart piece by piece and examined in an effort to determine the cause of death. A lot of information can be gleaned from the activities conducted inside this room, for example, the autopsy can show what types of incendiaries or chemical agents were being used by the enemy. Once all of the data is collected it is delivered to Commanders on the front lines to help them guard their units against future threats. The autopsy room was covered in stainless steel and white tile. Large drains are placed strategically in the floor to assist with drainage and even though there were no bodies in the room when we entered, fleshy remnants and hair could be seen clogging up in the drains, the byproducts of a recently conducted autopsy.

Off to the left from the autopsy area was the Final Prep room. Here, remains are placed in impeccably tailored service dress uniform, cosmetics and other aesthetics are applied and the service member is laid in repose in preparation for their family's viewing. As I made my way through the room, I saw a young marine lying on a table; I was taken aback because he didn't look real, he looked like a mannequin. I moved closer to him and was astounded by the effort that had been made to make sure he looked his very best for his family. The technician applying the last of the ribbons to the Marine's uniform looked up at me, smiled and said, "Some of my best work. He was pretty bad. I had to do a lot of reconstructive work on this one. He took one in the face." I remember not knowing how to respond his prideful boast. I guess he was proud of his success, much like Derek and I were the day before upon finishing our instruction. I didn't understand why but somehow it made sense. I left the Port Mortuary that day never forgetting the things I had seen or experienced. I don't think a word was said during the ride back to the hotel. Strangely enough, the experience did make me a better instructor in the mortuary subject matter and I frequently shared my experience with my students.

I worked diligently over the next few years to master my instructing skills and looked forward to going to work every day. The shared experience at Port Mortuary caused Derek and me to become closer. We spent almost every waking moment together either at work, or out fishing in the Gulf of Mexico. But, alas the time had come for me to move to my next duty station. I received orders to go to Davis-Monthan AFB in Tucson, Arizona, a place I had never been and quite frankly, was not too keen on going to, until I found out that Derek was going there as well. This was going to be fun! Once again, I dutifully packed up the family and headed west. We were Arizona bound.

Photo from the collection *"Dignified Transfer"* © 2009 Air Force Mortuary Affairs Operations, www.mortuary.af.mil

CHAPTER 4
The Pain Begins

A Technical Sergeant and newly assigned to Arizona, I thought I was ready to make a difference in the world, I thought I had made it. I had finally arrived; I was excited to explore my new niche in the world. Well, it wasn't long before my experience teaching Readiness was noted by my leadership. They vetted me to accept a position in the Readiness and Mortuary section of the squadron. Initially, I performed only deployment related work, ensuring the troops headed out to the war had the appropriate gear, arranging their travel and making training available to them. I was always conducting or scheduling some type of training to prepare my squadron for deployments, besides having to train and deploy every other year myself. I remember feeling very proud to be in charge of a program that placed me in a close working relationship with the unit's leadership. Knowing that they had entrusted me with so much responsibility made me feel important. I was so caught up in all the responsibilities and meetings that I was required to attend; I very quickly forgot that part of my job was to take care of the fallen as the Mortuary NCOIC. It was an afterthought to me because it almost never happened. Famous last words, as I would soon find out.

Late one afternoon, I received a call as I was heading out of the office to go home for the day. I remember thinking, *"Great, another last minute deployment tasking, there goes my weekend."* The muffled voice on the line was from the base's Command Post. "Is this the Mortuary Affairs Office?" the voice asked. I paused for a moment and replied, *"Yes, go ahead."* The voice came back on the line "We have an active duty death to report." The phone fell silent. I felt a thousand emotions all at once. I was oddly excited, scared and worried but I collected myself long enough to take down the information being recited to me on the phone, and then set about making phone calls and filling out the necessary paperwork. The family was flying in the next day so I had to prepare the narrative briefing required for my Commander's purposes. After meeting with the family and hearing their wishes he and I would need to discuss funeral arrangements.

The next day, I met with the Commander, both of us in our service dress uniform, as was customary for this type of meeting. We drove to the designated place where we had agreed to meet the family. The family had relatives who lived semi locally and opted to stay with them as opposed to staying in a hotel. We arrived about an hour and a half after departing base because the home was embedded deep in the Arizona desert. We exited my truck, checked out each other's uniforms and knocked on the front door. A woman answered, she looked as though she had been crying for days. Her face and eyes were red and flushed; she wore her grief like an outfit. I immediately felt bad and my stomach churned, I wanted so badly to help alleviate the pain she and her family were feeling. I promised myself at that moment I would do everything in my power to make the family's suffering as minimal as possible, a task that in future endeavors gave me much pride, and also changed my life. We entered the home it was crowded with family members, on what I can only imagine felt like the worst day of their life. Their loved one had suddenly died while home on leave from the war zone. Master Sergeant Brice Glibben had been doing some work in the front yard and suffered a heart attack and with his home in such an austere location, medical services could not arrive in time to save him. I was struck to the core by the thought that he had survived the enemy, but was taken before his time by doing yard work. It didn't make sense to me. But, I have come to realize that death rarely makes logical sense. We met with the family for what seemed like hours, going over every detail, having them sign tons of paperwork, determining what type of casket they wanted, how they wanted him dressed, where the services where to be held, and if they wanted us to fly in anyone to attend. We dotted all the "I's", crossed all the "T's" and then began our journey back to base. The Commander asked me to coordinate the transfer of the remains from the coroner's office to the funeral home that the family had selected. As soon as I got back to the office I started making calls and arranging transport. I also arranged for the Commander and I to attend the post-autopsy inspection of the remains scheduled for the next day. This would allow us to provide instruction to the mortician on how to prepare the remains.

I got home late that night and fell into bed exhausted from the sheer mental strain of the day. The next morning I felt uneasy, I had never done a remains inspection before, and was very nervous about it. I arrived at work early and

I began feeling strangely excited and curious, a feeling that made me angry at myself. Why was I excited to go see a dead body? Why wasn't I sad? This was a family man who had sacrificed his entire adult life serving his country. And yet, I couldn't shake the feeling of curiosity and excitement for what I was about to do. I met with the Commander to discuss directions to the funeral home and the protocol he expected me to follow. He dismissed me and we both changed into our dress blue uniforms. Thirty minutes later we met in the parking lot to drive to the funeral home. I couldn't help but notice how the building was in a very run down part of town, in an area that some would say was undesirable. I disapproved of the funeral home's location; I felt it disrespectful to have our deceased service members prepared in such a seemingly bad location. The funeral home looked as if it had been there since the turn of the century. The building was laden with heavy red brick that had chunks of mortar falling out of the cracks, the front lawn was gray and dead (I failed to see the symbolism at the time) and the parking lot's asphalt had wide cracks with weeds sprouting through them in a sporadic pattern. We entered the main lobby, which looked as if it had been decorated by someone's grandmother in the 1970s. The room contained furniture upholstered in maroon and gold fabric; the windows were hung with heavy curtains that resembled thick corduroy. A straight laced blonde woman wearing a black pantsuit appeared from out of the back and introduced herself to us, and without warning, very promptly greeted each of us with a warm-hearted hug. The Commander and I were both very puzzled. She must have noticed our bewilderment and very quickly explained, "In my line of work, we don't shake hands, we hug. We never know when it's the last time we will see someone." An odd greeting for sure, but we played along. In hindsight, her hugs were always very comforting; it gave me something to look forward to.

She explained that the remains of our service member had arrived and they were awaiting our arrival before beginning the preservation process. She then led us back to the working area of the funeral home, a place most never get to see. But, we had to do our inspection and this was the only place to perform it in a dignified manner. She led us down a long hallway lined with empty caskets, we moved past the office areas and into a room that had plastic curtains for a door, the kind you might see in a butcher's shop, or in a warehouse freezer. I was not prepared for what I saw beyond the curtain. I turned the corner and entered the main preparation room; the room was filled with at least thirty bodies. Most were covered in thin, white sheets, but some were exposed as they were being worked on by the morticians. I saw old and young, withered and burnt. Some of the bodies had devastating injuries, worse than I had ever seen in any horror movie. As we moved past the dead, our guide stopped by a gurney in the center of the room and removed the sheet. There lay Master Sergeant Brice Glibben, he was grey and lifeless, His body was completely laid open from shoulder to shoulder and down to his belly button. The skin on top of his head had been removed and was lying on the table next to his exposed skull. I took a deep breath as I looked into his cold, dead eyes. I will never forget those eyes, they had fear in them. They were odd looking to me because they were dry and absent of any sheen. I must have zoned out because my Commander interrupted my daze. "You okay, Sergeant Jordan?" he asked. I promptly responded, *"Umm, yes sir. I'm fine."* We proceeded with the inspection. The mortician removed the top of the skull; it made a sound I will never forget. It reminded me of a bowl turned upside down on a table being picked up, a hollow sound as the air entered the cavity. We bent over and looked inside the skull to ensure that the brain had been removed and placed inside the body cavity with the other organs. We also examined the remains for any signs of decay. The Commander gave detailed instructions to our guide on how to prepare the body for viewing. We were then joined by the Funeral Director who went over in detail how she would proceed, explaining what materials she would use, and how she would apply cosmetics. The Commander was satisfied and set a time for the next inspection to take place. This is when we would quality-assure that her work had been performed within the parameters of the contracted agreement.

We left the funeral home and headed back to base, another car ride with no words spoken. That night I had a really hard time sleeping because every time I shut my eyes, I saw his eyes, dead and fearful. I contemplated my own mortality over and over. I could not undo the memories from the day, the images troubled me, but sometime throughout the course of that night, I convinced myself it was just a job and I had no right to feel anything. It was my way of coping, I pressed on. I didn't share my day with my wife, which was odd, because we had made a ritual of going over the day's events with each other every night. However, I got the distinct impression that she understood and she never pressed the issue. The next day, I went to the funeral home alone to perform the post-embalming inspection. I followed my training to the letter, I felt the bicep to ensure rigidity; if the bicep was stiff and rigid it was a good sign that the embalming was done correctly throughout the body. I flipped the remains on its side to examine the back. Blood often pools to the back and if missed it can leak into the casket during transport. He did have some blood pooling, so I instructed the mortician to hypodermically embalm these areas by injecting the blood pockets with embalming fluid. I then handed over the uniform that I had purchased and placed ribbons on prior to my arrival. I agreed to return later in the day to inspect the final preparation.

I arrived late in the afternoon to do the final inspection. MSgt Glibben had been laid in a heavy wooden casket in his full service dress uniform. The first thing I noticed was that the scared look his face that was present earlier had been replaced, he looked at peace, almost smiling, as if he knew something we didn't. I did a close inspection of the uniform and of his facial features. I lifted his flight cap to ensure that if the cap did fall off the cranial stitching would not be visible. The mortician had done an exceptional job. I only needed to adjust his ribbons slightly and run a lint brush over his uniform.

I left the funeral home that day with an odd feeling in my stomach. I had peered behind the curtain; I now had carnal knowledge of every man's worst fear, death. I stared at my own mortality, and now I was married to it. I had information normal mortals did not want. I remember thinking about my own funeral and if someone would take as good care of me as I had tried to do with MSgt Glibben. I had a long, dark, drive home. No radio, no phone, just the sound of my truck's engine, and the smell of my burning cigarette as I chain smoked on one after another. It was my drug of choice for that series of moments; it relaxed me and made me feel less anxious. When I arrived home my wife met me in the kitchen and asked how it went. I told her, *"It was ok."* I wanted so badly to share what I had seen but I hesitated. I can't share this with her and that really sucked because we shared everything. My marriage died a little that day and every day thereafter, I choose, at my own demise, to carry the burden of my pain alone.

23

Over the next week I attended MSgt Glidden's memorial services, arranged the funeral and travel for his remains. I saw a lot of heartache and despair at those ceremonies, and when they played Taps I almost lost it. *"But wait,"* I thought. *"Why am I mourning a guy I didn't even know?"* I was mad at myself, how could I let it get to me? I'm stronger than this. I kept telling myself, *"Just put it away, just put it away."* I finished all the paperwork, closed the case file and felt myself grow a little older, a little wearier, and a lot more cynical. A few weeks went by and I got notified that I would be deploying to Kuwait in a month. I needed to get my affairs in order. I immediately picked up the phone, called my wife and told her the news so she could make arrangements with her leadership. Because she is also active military we wanted to ensure she would not deploy while I was gone. She, as always, was understanding and handled everything allowing me to focus on getting ready to deploy again. Over the next few weeks, my time was spent training and preparing for the upcoming deployment to a little place they called "The Rock" in Kuwait.

CHAPTER 5
The Rock

I arrived at the airport with my family in tow, fully dressed in my desert camouflage uniform. I looked up and saw some of my team members and their families assembled near the ticketing agents. As with any military sendoff, there was an abundance of tears and strong handshakes from squadron leadership. My wife, true to form, was stoic and strong. She leaned in and whispered in my ear, "Keep it in your pants, big boy." We both laughed. I gave my kids long, heartfelt hugs, fighting back the tears, and then they were gone. One thing that really tugged at my heart was, as my wife left the terminal that day, I saw her wipe away a tear. I have never told her I saw this because she prides herself on being a strong, military woman, she sees shedding tears as a weakness. But I saw it and at that moment, I knew I had the best wife I could ever ask for.

The flight was an agonizing nine hours to Germany then another eight plus hours into Kuwait. Again my feet were swollen, so much so that I had to loosen my bootlaces. We arrived in country late in the afternoon, loaded up our gear onto a bus and started our trek to the base. Kuwait is a dusty, dirty, little country that reminded me of my time in Saudi Arabia. However, the Kuwaiti people seemed a lot freer, I saw females driving, and even showing their arms in public. This type of behavior would never be tolerated by women in Saudi Arabia. We arrived at base, met our leadership, and were presented our duty assignments. My reputation must have preceded me because I was assigned to run the sports programs at the fitness center. Additionally, I was also assigned as the on-call mortuary NCO. To this end, I was given a 1980's style beeper and told by my superintendent "Pray this doesn't ring." But if it did, I knew all too well what to do.

My first month in country was very slow and uneventful. I scheduled sports tournaments for coalition forces and prepped playing fields, monotonous stuff. One day, I felt a weird sensation on my side. I thought to myself, *"What the…?"* I looked down and it was the beeper vibrating. As I took it off my belt a number appeared on the screen. I rushed to my work center and dialed the number. It was the command post. "Is this Sergeant Jordan?" I replied, *"Yes it is. How I may help you, sir?"* The voice on the other end paused, as if he was talking to someone else nearby. "Umm, yeah, we have a HR (Human Remains) inbound and need you on the flight line in fifteen minutes to receive." I paused and responded, *"Yes sir. Is it an aircraft transfer or will I need to house the remains for the night?"* "I'm not sure." He said. "I'm working a turnaround flight but it doesn't look like the weather is cooperating. So, be prepared to house. Copy?" I responded in turn *"I copy, sir."* My mind started racing with all the things I must do in the next few hours. I became laser focused, got in my vehicle, grabbed my line badge, (required for entry into restricted areas) and headed to the flight line to receive the fallen. I arrived at base operations just outside the aircraft ramp and hastily parked my vehicle. It must have been an '86 Chevy cargo van gutted of everything but the driver and a passenger's seat. It made a very good transport vehicle because it had no windows in the rear and a great suspension.

Photo from the collection *"Dignified Transfer"* © 2009 Air Force Mortuary Affairs Operations, www.mortuary.af.mil

We took great care to keep our operations in a war zone very clandestine, even altering our routes and ensuring areas were cleared during transfers. This wasn't to cover up the cost of war, but to save others the mental strain of constantly being reminded of death. As I slid out of the van I saw a young looking captain emerge from the operations center, seemingly anxious and shaken. I approached him and rendered the proper salute, which he absentmindedly returned. He asked, "Are you Sergeant Jordan?" I nodded and said, *"Yes sir... Sir. Are you ok?"* He looked at me, almost through me, and said, "I'm not really sure, and I don't know that it's any of your business, Sergeant, but what I am sure of is we have a dead soldier in that plane, and nowhere to put him." I gave him a puzzled look and told him, *"Well sir, that's where I come in. I assure you I have complete control of the situation."* He seemed relieved and asked, "So you can house the remains for the night and possibly tomorrow?" I nodded, and said, *"Yes sir, longer if necessary. I have fully equipped coolers, new body bags, tags, paperwork, the whole nine sir."* He smiled, and responded, "Well, halle-fuckin lujia!" he continued, "Now you know he's someone's brother or son, so make very sure you take extremely good care of him." I looked at him dead in the eye and said, *"Sir, I do this for a living, I'll treat him like he is my very own brother... because he kind of is."* I then rendered him another salute and turned to head towards the aircraft.

I could see in the distance the C-130 aircraft parked in the receiving spot and I could just barely make out the flag draped transfer case, a sight familiar to most Americans nowadays, but at the time it was not something that was very widely seen. I stopped just short of the loading area to check my tires for foreign objects that get lodged in the tread and can wreak havoc on jet engines. Even though the aircraft was propeller driven, the Air Force takes FOD, or foreign object damage, very seriously. I approached the aircraft and asked the Crew Chief to spot me as I reversed the van as close as I could get it to the aircraft loading ramp. He agreed and I parked the van about two feet from the plane. I jumped out, chocked the wheels on the van and met with the Aircraft Commander. We had a short discussion about off-loading and then quickly loaded the transfer case into my van. I secured it to the floor so that it would not shift during transport. I was about to leave when I heard, "Sergeant, can I speak with you?" I turned around and noticed it was the Aircraft Commander, a Major, looking to be in his mid-thirties. I responded with, *"Of course sir, what can I do for you?"* He pulled me to the side of the van well out of earshot of his crew and said, "Look, it was pretty hairy leaving Iraq, and I had to pull some tricky maneuvers. So, I'm not so sure what condition he'll be in, can you check it out?" I nodded and said, *"No worries sir. I'll take care of everything. You get some rest and we'll have him ready when you call."* He responded, "Thank you Sergeant." And he left. I hopped into my van and took one last look in the back to ensure everything was secure. I had a distinct feeling I had forgotten something, but I shrugged it off as my mind was on the task at hand. I put the van in drive and started to pull away. But, the van just roared and wouldn't move. I was confused and thought, *"Great, the van breaks down now?!"* I tried again, more whining from the engine and no movement. I punched the steering wheel in disgust. All of the sudden, I heard a loud whistle; it was the Crew Chief walking toward me with his hands in the air. "Hey! How about you un-chock your wheels, Einstein!" he screamed. *"Oh, fuck! Dumbass, dumbass, dumbass,"* I repeated to myself under my breath. I jumped out and re-moved the wheel chalks, not making eye contact with anyone on the line. I was very embarrassed! I got back into the truck and sped out of there en route to the mortuary tent.

I traversed the ten-mile drive with my mind focused on the stupid mistake I had just made, tearing myself apart for the momentary lapse of common sense. As I arrived at the mortuary tent, a thought entered my head. *"How the fuck am I going to unload this by myself?"* I backed up to the door of the tent and spied an Airman walking close by. He looked exhausted and beaten from a hard day, but, I needed a hand, and I was an NCO. *"Hey, Airman, I need a hand over here!"* I shouted, and as any Airman does when a senior ranking individual asks them for help, he hightailed it to me. He said, "What can I do for you sir?" I told him, *"Look, I have to load this cargo into this tent. Then, I might need your help fur-ther."* "Not a problem." he chirped. I leveled with him, *"This is a fallen warrior and utmost care must be taken in off-loading this transfer case, ok?"* His face fell. "What, sir?" *"Yes, it's a casket with a body in it, and I may need you to help me re-ice him for transport. Do you think you can handle that?"* "Umm, yes, sir," he said with a quivering voice. We began to un-strap the transfer case and off-loaded it into the tent and onto a large stainless table I had prepositioned in the center of the room. We removed the flag, unbuckled the locks on the case, and the smell hit us immediately. It was the stench of burned hair and flesh, a smell you never forget. It reminded me of rotten meat with a very distinct burnt plastic essence, much worse than my other encounters with death, as those were in a much more clinical setting. As we lifted the lid I noticed the body bag had a large rip from the shoulder down to the middle of the body. I could not see inside the bag but there was very definitely a large hole in the bag. I told the Airman to meet me outside because I needed to decide how to handle this. We went outside and had a cigarette as I pondered what to do next. I spoke with him at length and told him he could leave if he wanted to and that I would get someone else if he couldn't handle it. He agreed to stay but I could tell he was nervous and scared. I saw in his eyes a deep pain, somewhere between frightened and embarrassed. I knew he had just faced his own mortality, and it was my fault. A hot feeling rushed over me. I took a long drag from my cigarette, trying to make it last forever, rather than face the inevitable. I didn't want to do this to this kid, but I saw no other way.

We finished our cigarettes and went back into the tent. No words were spoken, just fleeting glances as we put on protective gear. I moved over to the transfer case, undoing the tags, taking great care to make sure that they were preserved and then I unzipped the bag. Inside was a white liner bag stained with blood and a matching rip, identical to the one on outer body bag. As I slowly unzipped the inner liner, the smell increased tenfold. It traveled up my nostrils and landed on my tongue making me gag. There's no other way to describe it; it smelled like death. As the remains became visible, it looked to be a burn victim. His face was melted and devoid of any hair with patches of bright red spotting the black charcoal looking skin. His eyes were cold and dark; his eyelids were completely burned off. This was one of those things that took me by surprise, as I could see the entire eyeball, it was very unsettling. Just then I looked up and saw the airman with his mouth wide open in shock. I asked him, *"Are you okay, man?"* He stared at me in silence for a moment and said, "Just never seen a dead guy before, sir." I responded with, *"It's an unfortunate part of life, son, but he died serving his country. So we must take great care to ensure he gets home as quickly and as dignified as possible. So you see, we cannot let him arrive in a ripped body bag, floating in bloody ice."* He nodded and I gave him detailed instructions on how we were to proceed. Once we removed him from the bag, we placed him into another bag and liner we had positioned on the stainless steel table in the center of the room. As we placed him in the bags some of his burned skin had adhered to our gloves and uniform sleeves, the airman looked at me and asked, "What do we do now?" I shrugged and told him, *"I'll figure something out."* We then secured both bags, reattached the tags and drained the fluids from the transfer case and sanitized the entire area. We placed the fallen back into the transfer case and re-iced his remains. Then we reattached the flag to the outer part of the transfer case and placed him into refrigeration. We put our gear, including our uniform tops, in red biohazard bags and set them aside to be turned in for disposal. Just as I was ready to release the airman and go decompress, I received another message on my God-awful beeper. I got to the nearest phone and it was base operations again. A flight had become available to transport our fallen hero home. I breathed a large sigh of relief and asked the airman to help me load the transfer case up into my van. He agreed and even insisted on seeing the task through to completion. We loaded the fallen and began the journey back to the airfield. As usual, not a word was spoken. All that could be heard was the sound of the overworked engine and the weak straps rattling in the back.

We arrived at the new aircraft, met with the Aircraft Commander and briefed him on our ordeal. I also explained that with such a quick turnaround, I hadn't had the time to fill out the appropriate paperwork. He told me not to worry; he had all the paperwork he needed. We secured the remains in the back of the aircraft, turned and rendered a final salute. Then he was gone.

I don't think I will ever forget the images I saw that day, nor the scared look on the face of the airman who assisted me. I never got his name, or maybe I just don't remember it. In retrospect, I wish I had. That night I missed home more intensely than ever, I sat near the perimeter of the base overlooking Kuwait City in the distance. Occasionally I could see what appeared to be mortars lighting up the sky over Iraq just miles away. I sat there and chain-smoked nearly all night listening to my iPod replaying a song my daughter had deemed as our song *"When You're Gone"* by the band Three Doors Down. Emotions overwhelmed me and for the first time in my career I wondered, *"Why? Why am I here? Why did he have to die? Just why?"*

Over the next few months I spent most of my time working in the fitness center, scheduling sporting events and the occasional trip into town to set up local events. The beeper would go off occasionally, but mostly for aircraft transfers and a few times for re-icing. I became cold to it, and trained myself to put those events in a place inside my mind where they didn't matter. They didn't happen; I was just doing my job. I finished my time in Kuwait and returned home to my loving family who missed me. But, I would sit up at night, haunted by visions of that day, the burned wrinkled skin, the bloody patches that contrasted against the charred flesh, the missing eyelids, and even worse, the fear in the airman's eyes, a fear I felt daily, I wanted to express that fear so badly. But, I couldn't, I had to be the rock.

Photo a derivative of *"The Rock Sign"* © 2005 FlyTheMig29, thosewackyiraqis.blogspot.com

CHAPTER 6
The Bleeding Trailer

I returned to work in the Readiness and Mortuary office after several weeks of leave and R&R (rest and relaxation) time. I was eager to get back to a sense of normalcy, but truthfully, I spent most of my days dreading the next call. Several weeks of training squadron members for their next deployment, fixing gear, and performing day-to-day operations passed. Then, one day the phone rang, I almost jumped out of my skin. I stared at it, and wished it away. I waited so long that it nearly vibrated itself off the table. Finally, I picked it up. "This is the base command post, is this on-call mortuary NCO?" I paused and said, *"Um, yes... I am he."* "We have an active duty death report. Are you ready to copy?" This routine had become old hat to me, I copied down all the information and I proceeded to gather the necessary paperwork to brief my Commander. The only information I had at the time was that it was a motorcycle accident and the member had been killed instantly. The family was from out of town and was notified of his death via personnel in their immediate area. I instantaneously started making assumptions about how he died, and what things he must've been doing wrong, I questioned why he had to ruin my day, my month. I was downright pissed off.

The next day I contacted the Coroner's office and then the funeral home to discuss transportation of the remains between the two. I had not yet gotten approval from the family to use the contract funeral home, but I wanted to get a jump on things. The deceased's mother and father had driven all night and had just arrived in the local area. I arranged for them to meet with my Commander to discuss funeral options. We agreed to meet the next day just after lunch; they were staying at a nearby Army post roughly 45 minutes from our base. The next day seemed redundant, I met the Commander, and we drove to the residence, got out of the car and knocked on the door. Then it changed, I remember vividly the first time I met the mother and father of the deceased. They looked to be in their early 60s and of Hispanic descent. The father was a shorter man, but I could tell by his mannerisms he was a very proud man. He had jet-black hair that was peppered with gray and a face withered by the years. He met us at the door with a very strong handshake. He put forth a brave face, but I could tell the news of his son's death had rattled him to the core. Trying to hide the tears, he asked us, "Please come in and have a seat." As we moved across the room, we saw the mother appear. She had a very kind and gentle face that reminded me of my own mother. Not necessarily in appearance, but in her demeanor. I instantly felt loved around her; she greeted us, not with a handshake, but with a hug. It hurt my heart to see these two individuals in so much pain. I wanted to reach out to them, wanted to tell them it would be okay. But, I couldn't, my job was to be a stoic, an unbiased symbol of strength. I had a duty to help them carry their pain, at least that is what I thought. As we discussed the funeral arrangements and the details for the viewing, the parents told us stories of their dearly departed son, SSgt Mitchell Trigger. They told us about the kind of person he was and how he had just spoken to them minutes before he died. He'd been riding his motorcycle up in the mountains, taking pictures, stopping nearly every hour to call his parents to tell them what an exciting time he was having. The entire family had a love affair with motorcycles and they were curious to know what he had been wearing at the time of his death. It was as if they were trying to find a reason for this tragedy, an explanation for why this might have happened. The Commander briefed the family thoroughly and decisions were made. Once all of the paperwork was signed we stood to take our leave. The mother stopped me for one last hug and as I leaned forward to hug her back, she lightly cradled my face with both her hands; almost as if she wanted to make sure I looked deep into her eyes. Then she said to me, "Please, find my son's camera and bring it to me." I was taken aback by her request; I didn't quite know what to say. So, I went to the military standard response, *"Yes, ma'am."* This made me feel uneasy because it's a cardinal rule: don't promise anything you can't deliver. A sentiment my Commander echoed to me on the ride home. I felt terrible and hardly slept that night, tossing and turning, my mind racing to plan an attack in the hopes of finding this camera.

I arrived at work the next day and immediately contacted the Summary Courts Officer, the person we assign to handle all of the personal belongings and legal matters for the deceased. I asked about the camera. He told me that he had not found a camera at SSgt Trigger's work center but that he would be heading over to his residence later that day to secure and inventory his household belongings. He would call me the moment he found anything. I was relieved, but lingering in the back of my head was one thought, *"What if he couldn't find it? What was I going to do? How would I deliver this news to SSgt Trigger's mother?"* I pushed these fears to the back of my mind and concentrated on arranging for transportation of his remains from the coroner to the funeral home, and scheduling the standard inspections. I now had a full report of the accident lying on my desk, which I reviewed so that I could efficiently prepare the Commander for his future meetings with the family. According to the report, Mitchell had come from the mountain into Tucson and had joined a motorcycle formation taking the far left position of four riders. He was familiar with these riders and they discussed the day's activities as they rode down a busy street. The group he had joined was heading to a local bike apparel shop to check out the sales, and possibly get some new gear. However, Mitchell was eager to get home so he could upload his pictures from the day and send them to his parents. As the group turned into the bike apparel parking lot Mitchell continued straight. A car that had been waiting at the next intersection to cross the busy street saw the majority of the formation turning and assumed Mitchell was turning too. The car entered the intersection, allowing no time for Mitchell to stop. Mitchell hit the driver's side door traveling approximately 45 mph. He was killed instantly by the impact, which fractured his skull, causing severe brain hemorrhaging and severing his spinal cord. The report cited that Mitchell had been wearing a helmet and full Kevlar reinforced riding leathers. Unfortunately, the impact was just too violent. Just then I thought back to the camera. *"He must have had it on him when he died!"* It was a greatly welcomed eureka moment. I immediately called the funeral home and told them that the second he arrived they needed to secure the camera from his personal effects, and call me so that I could retrieve it, clean it up, and return it to the family. Next, I went down the hall to brief the Commander and to let him know about my camera theory. Incidentally, he was unavailable, which made me feel let down. I wanted to share with him that the camera had been found, well, at least in my mind it had been. I went back to my office and started working on case notes. I was in the middle of arranging an escort for the remains to the burial site when the phone rang. It was the funeral home calling to report that they had not found a camera among SSgt Trigger's personal effects.

All at once, my fears were realized. I was going to have to give more bad news to the family. I was also a little relieved that the Commander had not been in to hear me gush about finding the camera prematurely. My head fell into my hands; I must have just been a pitiful site because one of my co-workers asked, "Are you ok?" I quickly shook it off and said, *"Yep, just a little tired that's all."* But I wasn't tired, I was crushed. I had to move on, I could not dwell on my earlier missteps, and I needed to focus on the present.

I made arrangements with the funeral home to view the body later that day and then contacted the Commander to brief him on the appointment time. He agreed to meet me at the funeral home. As I was driving to the funeral home from the base, I received a call. It was the father of the deceased inquiring on the status of the camera. I told them I had not located it yet, but I had some unturned stones to check and I would get back to them as soon as I had more information. I was very careful not promise anything this time. As I ended the conversation with him he said, "There is just one more thing. His riding leathers, we would like to have them too." He went on to explain to me the sentimental importance that they had to all the riders in the family. I explained to him in the simplest way possible that it was unlikely that the leathers would be salvageable due to medical treatment and the sheer violence of the accident. He asked me to do what I could and that he understood if it wasn't possible. So, now, not only do I have to track down a nonexistent camera, I also had to secure riding leathers that were more than likely mangled and bloodied. I sighed and hung up the phone, trying to be as professional as possible. In a burst of anger I repeatedly punched my dashboard until my knuckles bled. I wasn't mad at him, I was frustrated with myself. *"Why did I care so much?"* I thought to myself. Other people I knew would have just told him it couldn't be done, and that would be that. I, on the other hand, lived my life by a simple, guiding, philosophy: Treat the bereaved like they are part of your family. Sort of a mortuary *"golden rule"* if you will.

I entered the parking lot of the funeral home and saw my Commander waiting for me by the front door. I left my vehicle and greeted him with the appropriate customs and courtesies, which included a salute and a salutation. He returned the salute and held the door for me to enter. We were immediately greeted by the funeral home staff and shared a customary hug with each other. The Funeral

Director led us to the back where SSgt Trigger's remains were being kept. I prepared myself for the grizzly state that I thought the deceased would be in, after succumbing to such a violent death. What I saw was quite the contrary, on the table laid the remains of a young man in his mid-twenties with very minimal damage to his body. There was bruising around his neck but no abrasions or massive tissue damage like I had expected. The only real damage that I could see was from the autopsy incisions. We went on about our duties inspecting the remains and decided that an open casket could be an option for the family if they wanted it. The most remarkable characteristic of SSgt Trigger's remains were that his eyes seemed tightly closed as if in his last moments he was bracing for the impact of the crash. For this I was grateful because the eyes always got me. I was literally staring death in the face and the images always left an indelible mark upon my soul. We left the room to discuss how to proceed with the embalming. I asked the Funeral Director about the condition of SSgt Trigger's leathers. She stated that with the exception of where the hospital had had to cut the pants in order to remove them from SSgt Trigger's body, they were in pretty good shape. I told her about the family's request, she left the room and returned with the leathers in a paper bag. I grabbed the bag and looked inside. Everything was in order. She told me she searched again and even called the coroner but that there was no sign of the missing camera.

By then it was late in the day. The Commander and I decided to retire for the evening. We scheduled our inspection for the next day and left. I knew the family was eager to get the leathers, but I had to examine them to ensure there was nothing that might cause the family distress before returning them. Normally, I would drop this bag off at work before heading home but I decided, with the camera not being found, the least I could do was to get the leathers back to the family first thing in the morning. I decided to scrutinize them at home and clean them if necessary.

When I arrived at home I dropped the bag of clothes in my garage and went in to change out of my uniform, grab a beer and a cigarette to calm my nerves. I went out back to smoke and have my beer when I noticed my neighbor, Larry, barbecuing in his back yard, also with beer in hand. He came over to my shoulder high fence, leaned in and said, "What's going on man?" Larry had been my sounding board for everything from disappointing sports losses, to family problems. We had a ritual of commiserating over a beer or two nightly. Larry was an avid motorcycle rider and had raced his motorcycle semi-professionally in the past. I confided in him what was going on in the case and asked his advice on how to best clean the leathers. He agreed to help and told me after dinner he would stop by and lend a hand. Needless to say, I was relieved, as I had no clue how to clean leather. As promised he stopped by and we both went into the garage. I had my own motorcycle trailer parked on the far right side to keep it out of the weather. We laid the leather gear and helmet out on the trailer and inspected the contents there was nothing in any of the pockets and very minimal blood on the leathers. The helmet, on the other hand, was covered in blood inside and out. We determined the best way to clean the leather was to wipe it down with towels and bleach, but the helmet had to be totally submerged in bleach solution and water before being washed off thoroughly. Once we completed the task I laid out the gear on my trailer overnight to dry. I shook Larry's hand, bid him goodnight, and after a lengthy hot shower, I collapsed into bed. That night I dreamt of myself riding my own motorcycle and taking pictures at different stops. I distinctively remember putting my camera in my saddlebags after each stop. When I awoke the next morning it dawned on me, *"Of course! SSgt Trigger probably stowed the camera on the bike, in some type of a compartment, before the accident occurred."*

I was excited, to say the least! I went into the kitchen to make my morning coffee and as I had my back turned, I heard my daughter's voice behind me, "Daddy?" I turned and smiled but noticed she seemed scared. I leaned into her and said, *"What's the matter baby girl? Did you have a bad dream?"* She shook her head no. *"Well then, what's wrong?"* She looked up at me and said something I will never forget, "The trailer is dying." I was puzzled. *"What do you mean baby?"* She started to cry a bit and said, "I went to the garage to get a juice from the refrigerator and the trailer is bleeding." My skin went numb; chills raced up my spine. I thought, *"Oh my God! What have I done?"* I told her *"Daddy was painting and it must just look like its bleeding, but sweetheart, trailers can't bleed."* She smiled and went back to her room to get ready for school. I was mortified! I just let the most innocent creature in the world see my horror;

it was one of the worst moments in my life. I grabbed some towels and went to the garage. Sure enough, during the drying process the helmet had drained residual bleaching fluid out from inside the helmet, and had run down the side of the trailer, collecting in a puddle on the floor. The fluid had a red tint to it, so I could see why she came to the conclusion that it was dying. I got the bleach out and cleaned up the floor and placed all the bloody towels in a trash bag so I could properly dispose of them on the base. I got dressed and headed into work.

My mind was fixated on the day's tasks. I was determined to find the camera. I arrived at work and contacted the tow yard where the motorcycle was taken after the accident, I also arranged to meet the Summary Courts Officer there, so that if the camera was on the motorcycle, he could witness me removing it for return to the family. When I arrived at the tow yard the Summary Courts Officer and I went to the front office and asked to be led to the back of the yard where the bike was housed. It was a red sport bike, the kind of motorcycle more popularly known as a "crotch rocket". My stomach fell, no saddlebags. I started thinking, *"Where would I put a camera if this were my bike?"* It hit me like a bolt of light-ning, *"Under the seat."* I quickly found the seat release and sure enough, there was the camera! I let out a loud sigh and inspected the camera. All the pictures from that day were still there. I was so relieved. Not only did I have the camera but I had his leathers too. The Summery Courts Officer entered the items on his inventory and placed an entry into his log. I arranged a meeting with the fam-ily and returned the items they had requested. There was a sense of happiness in that room, a room once filled with sorrow. I was proud of being able to bring these items to them. As I left the family's residence that day, I looked back over my shoulder and I saw a husband holding his wife in his arms, as they shared the last moments of their son's life and they cried happy tears. I returned to the funeral home and executed my final inspection. As always, the Funeral Director had done an amazing job preparing SSgt Trigger for viewing. He looked peace-ful and proud in his dress uniform. The only thing left to do was to get him to his hometown for the funeral that was scheduled to take place in three days. I went back to the office, made all the arrangements and effectively closed the case file on SSgt Mitchell Trigger. One issue still lingered, the discussion with my daughter that morning is something I never shared with anyone… not even her mother. To this day, my daughter has never brought it up again. I would like to think she doesn't remember it, but it's something that haunts me, "Daddy, the trailer's dying."

CHAPTER 7
The Disgruntled Wife

It had been a couple of months since I had closed the motorcycle case and I was busy with the base exercise. We were practicing for an upcoming inspection. These exercises were never fun. We spent hours training in the field in full chemical warfare gear. There were sirens, smoke grenades, simulated explosions and even role players posing as terrorists storming the base. I get it; we needed to practice for the real thing, it just all seemed so contrived and overdone. I think anyone that has ever served in a military uniform will agree with me, these exercises are redundant. During one day in particular, I was in the middle of instructing a self-aide and buddy care class on how to properly treat combat injuries. The mortuary cell phone rang; it was the command post with a death message. Apparently, this was a heart attack victim. I was relieved because that meant there would be no mitigating circumstances. He died in his sleep at home, it sounded pretty straightforward to me.

I called the Commander, briefed him and set up a replacement to take my place in the exercise. Next, I contacted the family and we agreed to meet the next day at their home to discuss funeral arrangements. While I read the report the only thing that seemed odd to me was that the deceased was only 38 years old. The Commander and I both thought this would be an easy case to work with no perceived challenges. By now, the mortuary business was beginning to feel like old hat to me. I had a system of case management that had gotten me a lot of accolades both from families I had dealt with and my leadership.

I arrived the next day in my battle dress uniform but had my dress blues in tow for my meeting with the family later that day. As I settled in at the job for the day, I noticed a small envelope on my desk addressed to me. This was odd. I typically did not receive mail at work. The envelope contained a card with a picture of a man in uniform on the front that looked very familiar to me, but I could not place him. I opened the card and immediately realized who the man was. It was the man I had just buried that had died in a motorcycle wreck, Mitchell Trigger. The card was a thank you note from the family telling me how appreciative they were of all my hard work on their son's funeral. I smiled and a sense of pride overcame me. I decided to display it proudly on my desk so that everyone could see how well I did my job. It is something we do in the military; we revel in our own accomplishments. As the day went on, I caught myself staring at the card frequently, looking at the man on the cover, so full of life, so happy and proud. I had not known him before his death, so I spent a good amount of time imagining him as a living person, almost obsessively. I moved it from my view and placed it on the top of my desk credenza, out of my direct sight. During the next several years, the card traveled everywhere with me. It was almost as if I was holding on to his memory, I can't explain why I carried it, I just needed it.

The Commander rang my line and asked to confirm the time of the meeting with the family. He also wanted to ensure that I had all of their paperwork in order. I jokingly replied, *"Come on sir, you know me better than that."* He chuckled and we agreed to meet an hour before the scheduled time to ride together to the residence. Normally, I would drive and he would navigate via the map I had printed out. But this particular family lived very close to my own home, so I was already familiar with the area. During our ride to the home, the Commander asked me questions about local landmarks and businesses, he very rarely left the base due to his demanding schedule. I found this comical and would rib him about it frequently.

We arrived at the home, put on our game faces, walked up and rang the doorbell. We were greeted by a pre-teen boy who didn't seem to understand what was going on. We told him who we were and asked to see his mother. She was sitting at a round dinner table in the rear of the home near a sliding glass door that led to the back yard. She was smoking and looked like she hadn't moved in days. She asked us to have a seat, we complied and just as the Commander began to speak, she interrupted in a stern voice and said, "Look, I don't trust the military, therefore I don't trust you." Staring directly at my Commander, I could tell he was visibly shaken. Commanders are not accustomed to any form of disrespect but she wasn't military so he had to sit there and tolerate her wrath. I sat wide-eyed, hoping she wouldn't direct her rage at me, but she continued with her verbal assault. "I was in the military for 15 years. I fell off a ladder while working on one of YOUR planes and broke my back. I can no longer work and all I got from the god-dammed military was 30 percent disability. So you can probably understand my distrust of commissioned officers." Surprisingly enough, my Commander took it all in stride; he made her feel at ease and went on with his briefing without a hitch. He then assured her that he would have little or no contact with her and explained that he was placing me in charge of the case so she could feel more at ease. I was floored both by the fact that he was so trusting of my abilities and that she was going to allow it. He finished the briefing, got all of the paperwork signed and we started to leave. As we stood up, she stopped me, "Sergeant Jordan, I want him buried in his battle dress uniform. He worked for a living and hated fucking blues." I smiled, because I think we all have shared that feeling. She went upstairs to gather his things as the Commander went to the vehicle. I waited at the bottom of the stairs; she reappeared in a few minutes later, uniform and boots in hand. She looked around as if to ensure the Commander was out of earshot, and then stared directly into my eyes. I could tell she was holding back tears. She grabbed my arm, her lips quivered and said, "Take care of him, please take care of him." I looked back at her, put my hand on hers and told her, *"Look, he is in the best hands he could be in. I make it my business to make sure of that. Don't worry."* She smiled a half smile like she wanted to trust me, but I could tell she was still apprehensive. I took my leave from her and entered the vehicle. As I buckled my seat belt I looked over at the Commander and said, "So much for an easy case." He looked back at me and said something that resonated with me for years "Sarge, opportunities present themselves in many different ways. Its how you embrace them that matters." It was if he was handing me the torch and honestly, it felt good. Not good that someone had died, but good that my Commander recognized and appreciated my knowledgeable expertise. I went home that night excited, almost giddy to share the news with my wife. But, by the time I got to the house, she had already gone to bed. So I opened a beer and retired to the back porch because I was sure Larry would be out doing the same. I always looked forward to talking to him after a long day at work.

We went through a good amount of beer that night, an occurrence that had become very typical, as I had been numbing my pain with alcohol. Larry was the best kind of drinking buddy, no judgments, no sarcasm; he just listened and offered opinions when asked. I retired sometime after midnight and tossed and turned most of the night. I began to question my ability to pull this one off. It was my first cremation and I was shaken by the possible mistakes I might make.

The next day, I made all the usual arrangements with the funeral home and set up the inspection for later in the afternoon. I also arranged to inspect the crematory to ensure it met standards. It would also allow me the opportunity to answer any questions about the process the wife may have. I arrived at the funeral home and met with our Funeral Director. She administered the standard hug and led me back to the prep room. I didn't expect anything too startling but as I entered the room, I saw something that almost doubled me over. Directly to my right on a table was a small female child no more than four or five years old, burnt so badly from the sun, her skin appeared purple in color. She had the most horrifying look on her face, and it made me stop in my tracks. I immediately asked, *"What happened to her?"* The Funeral Director moved to the body quickly and covered her and told me, "Oh, she was an illegal trying to cross the border with her family. Her mother and father are over there." She pointed to the far end of the room. At that moment I had a flash of my own daughter lying on that table. It scared the shit out of me! I could see it vividly; it began to haunt my every thought. I tried to shake it off and move onto our deceased service member. As expected, there was not a whole lot of damage to his remains just typical post-autopsy incisions. Since this was a cremation no embalming had to be done. I just had to ensure he was dressed in the uniform that the wife had requested. I handed the uniform to the mortician and she placed it on the table and asked if I would like to tour the crematory while her staff dressed the remains. I agreed.

We left the building and entered the crematory in the rear of the complex. It was an old white building with steel doors. As we entered I saw the two ovens referred to as "retorts." Then, the Funeral Director began to explain the process to me. The body would be placed into a wooden casket minus the brass ornamentation, which would be turned over to the family. Next, the casket would be placed into a retort and burned at high temperature for two to four hours depending on the size of the body. She then took me into the next room where there was a machine affixed with two large wheels resembling the drums on a steamroller, only much smaller. She explained to me that after cremation the bones are left and they would be run though these drums to be pulverized. She then showed me some remains after this process and I was shocked. The box was the size of a shoebox and contained tiny bone fragments. It resembled kitty litter. I had always thought ashes where more fine in texture. She explained to me that they could be run through again if a finer texture was requested. One of the boxes had a metal piece in it that looked like the grated drain stop in most stainless steel sinks. She told me that was a knee replacement and would be offered to the family. I asked her, *"Why would anyone want that?"* she replied "Its titanium. Most families request everything from dental fillings to the hardware inside the bodies to melt down either for cash or memorial jewelry." I shook my head; the concept was unsettling. Just then, my mind flashed back to the autopsy room. I kept seeing my daughter on the table in my mind's eye. Again, I shook my head trying to get the images out of my brain, but to no avail.

I left the building in a hurry and lit a cigarette hoping it would calm me down, but it did not work. The Funeral Director came outside and told me that I would be visiting her if I didn't quit smoking soon. I smiled, and she walked me back to the room where our service member was. He was dressed and they even applied make up to his face in case the family wanted to see him prior to cremation. I looked over his uniform and everything looked in order. I stepped outside to call the deceased's wife to give her an update. When she answered, she told me to go ahead and proceed with the cremation. I gave the instruction to the Funeral Director. We then agreed on a time to meet the next day so I could be there for the loading of the retort. I went home that night not being able to shake the image of my daughter on the table out of my head. It scared me; I must have driven 100 mph just to hold her in my arms. When I arrived home I hit the door with fury and called out her name, *"Summer, Summer!"* She appeared around the corner and I scooped her in my arms and held her as tightly as I could without hurting her. The visions subsided for the time being and I retired to the patio for my nightly drinks and chat with Larry. Since that day a strange thing has happened to me. Anytime I meet new people, if I look in their eyes, I can see them on the table in the preparation room. For this reason, I don't make a lot of eye contact anymore.

The next morning my wife told me some more troubling news. She said I was screaming in my sleep. I didn't give it too much thought at the time. I just thought it was a bad dream, which I had no recollection of, so it didn't give me too much need for concern. But this is the first time I recall my wife begging me to go to my Commander and reassign my position, an idea I was very dismissive of. My wife had suspected for some time that this job may have been affecting my mental well being, but I never gave it a second thought. I had a job to do and I was good at it, so no one was going to tell me otherwise.

I arrived at the funeral home and inspected the coffin to ensure the remains were inside and still dressed appropriately. Everything checked out so we loaded the coffin into the retort, shut the door and turned on the oven. As I left the building I noticed there was no smoke coming from the stacks atop the building. The Funeral Director explained to me that the ovens burn so hot that smoke is not produced. I said, *"You learn something new every day."*

Over the course of the next several days the widow confided in me her constant battles with the government trying to get her disability rating increased, her overall displeasure with anything that had to do with the military, and how she felt so disregarded by the system. We also discussed the memorial service that had been arranged inside a hanger at her husband's squadron. She was apprehensive about attending as she felt her disdain for the military may cause her to do something that may dishonor her husband's memory. I spent a lot of time with her, mostly listening to her rant and assuring her that I would be there to play defense if she needed to me to.

The day of the memorial arrived. I called the funeral home to pick up the urn containing the service member's ashes so that it could be displayed at the memorial service. The wife had decided not to have a traditional burial service. The memorial in the hanger would have all the elements of a burial service to include honor guard and a bagpipe player. I arrived at the funeral home and picked up the urn. It was an oak box, smaller than a shoebox with a gold plaque inscribed with his name and the dates of his life on it. In the center of the plaque was the Air Force Symbol. I carried it out to my truck and it struck me, *"How am I supposed to transport this?"* I stood there for a moment, as I couldn't just put it in the back seat to roll around and possibly damage it. I decided the best thing to do would be to put it in the passenger seat and strap it in using the seat belt. Amazingly it worked very well although it was awkward. I made the trip to base and, as I was going through the gate, the guard informed me that I had to pull over, as my vehicle was being randomly searched. I tried to explain my situation to the guard, but he insisted so I pulled over, got out, and waited for the other guard to proceed to my truck. I explained the situation to him and he looked at me puzzled. I opened the passenger door and showed him the urn. He turned to me and said in a somber voice, "You can go, sir." I proceeded to the hanger slightly amused, as these things seem to happen to me a lot.

I entered the hanger through the side door and asked where the family was being staged prior to the service. A young airman who was working in the building pointed me to an office just up the hallway. I walked to the room, knocked on the door and was met by the wife. I explained to her I had the ashes in the truck and requested direction on where she would like me to place them. She directed me to a table in the center of the hanger next to a very large picture of the deceased. I returned to the truck, retrieved the urn and placed it on the center of the table. As I turned to leave the area, I noticed the wife in the doorway. She looked as if she was holding back tears; I approached her and offered an ear. She declined, so I told her where I would be waiting during the service. I wanted her to be to be assured her husband's ashes were always under my watchful eye. She disappeared back into the family staging area. Guests had begun to arrive and were paying their respects to the urn, most of them in tears. I positioned myself in the back of the hanger behind the crowd. The hanger was massive and there must have been well over five hundred military and civilian attendees. It was not long before the service started. His Commander, the Chaplain, family members and co-workers all shared stories about him and then they played a video commemorating his life. I thought that was the end of the service but then, all of a sudden, the enormous hanger doors began to slide open on the flight line side. As they opened, an aircraft postured just outside the door came into view. Standing in front of it was the Honor Guard dressed in full ceremonial uniforms. Out of the silence a booming voice shouted, "READY. AIM. FIRE!" All seven members raised their weapons in perfect unison and fired into the sky. They repeated this action twice more, successfully completing a 21 gun salute. No sooner had the muzzle smoke cleared when the sounds of a bugler playing "Taps" began its mournful warble. Heart wrenching sobs from the crowd became audible. At this point I was struggling to keep my own emotions in check, when just to my left, the bagpipes began to play "Amazing Grace." The bagpipe player was dressed in full Scottish kilt and walked through the center of the hanger, parting the crowd as he played. He continued and walked out of the hanger doors still playing the music, the sound trailed off until it was a faint whisper. It was a very touching, memorial that left me speechless.

Attendants filed out as I secured the urn and went back to the family staging area to get directions from the wife on how she wanted me to proceed. She met me in the hall and asked me to place the urn inside the room. She would transport it home. I complied, and as I was leaving, she asked to see me in the hallway. She grabbed my arm, pulled me to the side, looked me in the eye and said "I had given up on the Air Force… until I met you." Her lip quivered. I held back my own tears and just nodded. I was at a loss for words. I left that day a changed man. The case that promised to be easy proved to be anything but.

Airplane Hangar Sketch © Justin Jordan

CHAPTER 8
The Hero

It was a weekend. The family and I had been enjoying the unseasonably nice weather camping at an ATV Park. It had been a long weekend of fun and we were just arriving back home. The sun had burnt and dehydrated all of us, and I was ready for a long hot shower. Just then my mortuary cell phone rang. This time it was my Commander. He told me there had been an incident in one of the local canyons and two of the base's personnel were missing after a flash flood. He asked me to prepare my search and recovery team by placing them all on standby. A search and recovery team is comprised of twenty-four volunteers from all units on the base. Their primary purpose was to recover human remains after an aircraft crash, a very tedious task, as sometimes only body parts and personal effects are found. I trained this team every three months to maintain proficiency, but the composition of the team was always changing due to deployments. Therefore, it was difficult for me to maintain a competent staff.

I would drill team members on grid searches, flanking, collecting, bagging and marking of remains. I had just finished with notifying team members when I turned on the news to learn that the two missing base personnel were a young, Special Operations Staff Sergeant and one of the civilian lifeguards employed by the base swimming pool. Apparently, they were hiking in one of the local canyons when the female waded out in ankle deep water to take a picture on a small sandbar in the middle of a dry creek bed. The Staff Sergeant was on shore snapping pictures when a flash flood whisked the lifeguard away. According to eyewitness reports, the Staff Sergeant, a trained Pararescueman, jumped into the raging waters in an attempt to save her. No one had seen either since.

I followed the story closely that night while doing numerous Internet searches, trying to keep abreast of any breaking news. I do not remember sleeping that night. I arrived at work the next day and made sure my team's gear was ready. Just after finishing my first cup of coffee, I got the call to mobilize the team. I sprang into action, calling the team to the rally point and arranging transportation to the area where the two individuals were last seen. I went directly to the rally and made a call to the on scene, Incident Commander for a situation brief.

Our rally point was a small warehouse tucked away in an austere location on the base. When I arrived, nearly half of the team had already mustered, and before I exited my truck, I was already barking orders to gather equipment. Once all the gear was prepared and the full team was assembled, I gathered everyone for their briefing. I had just started when my phone rang. I excused myself for a moment and answered. It was the On-Scene Commander calling to let me know that they had found the two missing individuals. Both were deceased and they were being transported to the local morgue for autopsy. He also gave the order to dismiss the search and recovery team and to stand down. Oddly enough, I felt disappointed. I was jacked, ready to use the knowledge that I had trained so many people dozens of hours to perform. I was also saddened that the two missing people were deceased, as I wanted the opportunity to find them alive. I dismissed the team and returned to my office. I now had a mortuary case to prepare.

Over the next few days, I gathered all the necessary paperwork and made arrangements for the transportation of the deceased. I worked closely with the Commander in setting up a meeting with the family to discuss the arrangements. By this time, I had seen almost every way to die and had become cold to the entire process. I still harbored feelings of despair, as this case once again, validated in my mind that no matter what you do you could be gone in an instant. The family had given permission to use our contract funeral home prior to their arrival. This was a first for me as typically we met with the family prior to any inspection of the remains. But, in a way, it was helpful as we could brief them on the condition of the remains during the initial briefing. This could possibly help them better decide on open or closed viewing and this, being a water death, promised to be very gruesome.

When the Commander and I arrived at the funeral home I noticed that the typical cars were not in the parking lot. I didn't give it much thought as we proceeded inside to meet with the staff. We met with the receptionist and she announced our presence. This time a very large man appeared to greet us, not the typical Funeral Director. We had seen him in the past and had made joking comments that he resembled the character "Lurch" from the television show *"The Addams Family."* As a matter of fact, that became our nickname for him. He led us down the back hall to the autopsy room. I couldn't help but be disappointed that we had not received our traditional hug greeting as we had become accustomed to from the female Funeral Director. We entered the room and noticed a particularly pungent smell. It was almost unbearable. It had the familiar death smell, but this one was particularly bad. It had a musty, almost rotten egg smell. As I hovered over the remains, I noticed the deceased was covered in abrasions, some small, some fairly large with pieces of tree branches embedded in the skin. As I scanned the body I looked to the head and I was awe struck. It appeared as though he had no eyes! Apparently, they had been gouged out of his head by the force of the water slamming his body into the trees that surrounded the canyon. I looked closer and noticed his eyes were not actually missing but in fact had been deflated. The membranes resembled a deflated balloon inside his eye socket. This now topped my list as the most gruesome thing I had ever seen. For the first time, I was nauseated and had to excuse myself. I had seen all I needed and had no instructions for the morticians, as the family was still en route.

That evening I rushed home. I was the coach of my son's football team and had a scheduled practice. I gathered my plan for that night's practice but could not shake the nausea. I asked my assistant coach to lead practice; he agreed without hesitation, as he too, was military and understood my job. I returned home but skipped the beer and late night talks with Larry and opted to go straight to bed. I tossed and turned that night but eventually fell asleep. This is the first time I can remember having vivid dreams about my experiences. In this particular dream, I was standing in the prep room in knee high bloody ice and looking in a mirror, screaming because I had no eyes. I screamed for what seemed like days and woke up in a cold sweat. My wife told me I had been talking in my sleep and she was worried about me. I wanted to tell her she was over-reacting but I had literally lost my voice. She was annoyed with me, because she thought I was ignoring her and stormed out of the room. I went into the bathroom and gargled with mouthwash enough to get my voice back to just above a whisper and ran out to explain to my wife what had happened, but she had already left for work. I continued to get ready for work and gradually my voice returned enough to speak in normal tones. I called my wife to explain but she was very busy and did not have time to discuss it with me. This time, the only thing she said to me was, "You need to get out of that job. It's killing you." I just scoffed at her and responded with a snarky, *"Whatever."* I couldn't fathom leaving my job. If I asked to be moved out of this job someone else would have to do it and I would not wish that on my worst enemy.

This case had had a lot of attention in the community because the local media was touting our deceased SSgt as a hero, losing his life to save another at the cost of both of their lives. I also felt bad because the Air Force did not offer any casualty assistance to the lifeguard's family because she was a part time civilian employee. Her family was left to handle everything on their own. I also felt angry at him for doing something so careless, but then my feelings wavered. I immediately felt a sense of guilt for my anger. This was someone who put another's life before his own, and without thinking, he made the ultimate sacrifice. Maybe it was jealousy mistaken for anger. Nevertheless, I completed the case and oddly enough I do not remember much more about him. However, the one thing that resonates in my mind is his blind heroism. Or is it that he was the hero with no eyes.

CHAPTER 9
The Party Murder

Months had gone by without a death on base and I had settled into a comfortable routine without the burden of the mortuary cell phone ringing. We had a new Commander who was a really down-to-earth guy. He liked sports and was very easy to talk to. He made us feel more like friends than subordinates. He also had the unique ability to make you understand when he was serious and when it was time for business. It was a Monday morning. I had just settled into my desk and had taken one or two sips of my morning coffee when the Commander walked into my office. We all jumped to our feet, as it is customary to do when a person of a certain rank enters a room. Most of the time he would place the room at ease immediately. But this time, he made a beeline for my desk, locking eyes with me at every step of the way. He asked me to follow him to his office. I complied and followed him out of the room. It was a short walk down the hall but it seemed to last forever. I silently wondered what I did wrong. I racked my brain trying to think of what I might have done to make him this upset.

Upon entering his office, I centered myself on the middle of his desk, standing at attention. He sat down in his chair, looked up at me and said, "Really, sit your ass down." He chuckled a bit. I turned to find a seat. He began to tell me about a young airman that had died the previous Saturday night at a party in Tucson. At the time the local authorities said it was due to a fight that had happened and that eyewitness reports cited the deceased as the provoker. I looked at him and must have had a bewildered look on my face, because he put his hand up as if to let me know not to talk and said, "I know you typically handle everything and you get the call as soon as someone dies. But, I felt you needed to enjoy your weekend." He continued, "Besides, the coroner was not going to be finished with him until this afternoon because it is a possible homicide." I was relieved and felt an admiration for him. This was the first time any of my superiors had shown an interest in my well-being.

He went on to brief me on the case and what his expectations were of me. I always appreciated it when a superior laid out expectations, because it was something I always did for my subordinates. He explained to me that the deceased was a young airman, approximately 19 years old, and his family was already en route. They would be staying at base lodging upon arrival. I felt weird, all of the things I normally took care of the Commander had done for me. I felt relieved and mildly pissed at the same time. I wondered if he did not trust in my abilities or maybe he was just being nice. In any case, I had my marching orders so I left his office and started on my preparations.

The next day we had set an appointment with the family just after lunch. The Commander and I dressed in our blues as was customary. We walked up to the door of the lodging room and were greeted by the deceased's sister. She was in her early twenties and looked visibly distraught. When she opened the door to greet us she said nothing, she merely pointed to the middle-aged Hispanic couple sitting on the couch. We moved past her and entered the room. The wife rested her head on her husband's chest as she wept. He was doing his best to hold back his emotions as he held her in his arms. I noticed the tear stains on his cheeks as I got closer. I think he knew I had noticed the evidence of his tears because he rushed to wipe his eyes as we came closer. I could tell he was a proud man who didn't like to show emotion; he needed to be the anchor of the family. Without a word we instantly understood each other.

The Commander introduced us and began to explain our purpose. He then reached out and held the mother's hand. I was floored! I had never seen someone in his position share such compassion. It made me respect him even more. Over the next hour, I learned about A1C Sean Campos, a California native that entered the military to escape the gang life that so many of his relatives had been involved in. His family was so proud of their son. He was determined to make a better life for himself. They talked about him with such reverence and pride. It made me feel proud to have served alongside him, even if I didn't know him. The family also expressed the anger they had toward the Air Force, as the initial reports were that he had been killed by other Air Force Members. They trusted no one and felt like outsiders on base. My Commander assured them we would do everything we could to make the process easier on them and offered them my cell phone number for them to call night or day to answer any questions they may have. We finished our meeting and left. I went directly back to the office to research the case to find out the specifics of the death. I typically did this as I felt it made me feel closer to the case and helped me answer questions that might arise.

What I read did not match the image I had in my mind after speaking to his family. The report told the tale of a young man who allegedly hit a female for resisting his advances. He was then approached by several other males at the party and a fight ensued. According to the report, he instigated the fight and those interviewed at the scene were released, due to the officer's determination that they all acted in self-defense. What puzzled me was he was found in the street by a third party. No one at the party called to report the death; they just left him where he laid. Something did not sit right in my mind, but my job was not that of an investigator. I had to be there for the family and I could not let my personal feelings interfere with my job performance so I pushed these feelings to the side and arranged for the series of inspections we had to do.

I arrived at the funeral home the next day and met the Commander in the parking lot. I briefed him about our mortician and her affection for hugs. He thought it was comical and went along with it. The Funeral Director met us and I introduced our new Commander to her, and before she could say anything he asked her for a hug. She laughed and said, "I see Sergeant Jordan has briefed you well." They both grinned ear to ear and embraced in a cordial manner. I took my turn and picked her off her feet and spun her around. I thought I would keep the levity going. It made the process a bit easier. It took the heaviness out of the room, even if for just a minute.

We entered the back room and I saw him on the table, the first thing that stood out to me was how much he reminded me of my son. His body structure, especially through the rib area, was very similar, in spite of the fact that my son was only 10 at the time. He was of small stature, no larger than 5'5" and couldn't have weighed more than 140 lbs. I also noticed he didn't have much of any bruising on his face and his hands weren't cut up like you would have expected from someone who just lost a fight for their life. This puzzled me so I asked the Funeral Director why these things were not apparent. She then asked me to look at the back of his neck. It was covered in bruises and cuts. She also removed his skull bones and showed it to me. It was in two pieces. She held it together and said, "Look at this hole." As she placed the two cracked pieces of skull together you could see a definite round hole in the very back. It reminded me of when someone hits a piece of plywood with a hammer. An indentation is visible, but it would splinter inward. I asked her what she thought had happened and she said in her opinion someone hit him in the back of the head with something like a hand held sledgehammer. Furthermore, she explained that skulls don't crack in half without severe force. I stood there contemplating this, no defensive wounds and severe posterior head and neck trauma? This kid didn't know what hit him. I thought to myself *"He was murdered."*

Unfortunately, I was not a law enforcement officer and had only opinions on what happened. Opinions I could never share as it was out of the scope of my job. I was horrified to think that this kid was jumped then beaten to death and he never saw it coming. No matter how socially unacceptable his actions may have been, he did not deserve to die in this manner. I returned to the office that day solely to look at the death certificate. I wanted to see for myself what the medical examiner cited as the cause of death. Sure enough, it was labeled as a homicide. I shook my head but told myself, *"These assholes are going to pay for their crimes."*

The Commander had scheduled another meeting with the family to discuss assigning an escort to Sean's remains for the trip home to California. On the way over I asked the Commander to consider assigning me to the duty of Military Escort. I had trained every escort in the last couple of years on the duty but had never served in the capacity. I felt it would enhance my abilities to do my job and that is how I sold it to him. Secretly, I felt sorrow for the family; I wanted to be there for them. During our meeting with the family, the Commander pitched the idea of me performing the task of escort and they agreed without hesitation. I now had a lot of work to do. I got on the phone with the airlines to arrange services with the airline's mortuary representative. We went over every detail meticulously; I even went so far as to call the supervisors at each layover to ensure that nothing would be left to chance. I was always floored when I called somewhere and told them who I was and what I did, how quickly they would respond with the correct phone numbers and contacts to ease my trouble.

Over the next few days the family left to arrange the funeral and I went about the business of preparing for our travel and ensuring Sean was well embalmed and dressed correctly. The day arrived for me to travel to California and escort the remains of Airman Sean Campos home one final time. I arrived dressed to the nines in my service dress uniform. The man we had come to know as "Lurch" was waiting for me near the rear of the funeral home. He had pulled up the hearse and went inside with me to do one last inspection of the remains. His uniform looked good and his makeup was also done expertly. I checked the paperwork and the shipping container to ensure everything was correct and we began to load him in the hearse. As we were doing this, the Funeral Director came in and gave me her cell phone number. She told me that if I had any problems to call her day or night. I couldn't imagine anything that I would need to call her about, but it was a nice gesture. We left for the airport and arrived in the shipping area back where all the mail planes are parked. We met with the shipping coordinator and loaded Sean's remains on a luggage tug to be transported to the aircraft. I inspected the tug thoroughly before locking the netting shut with zip ties. I had to clear airport security and did not want anyone messing with the shipping container in the brief time I was away.

The airport staff rushed me through security and plane-side in less than fifteen minutes. As I was arriving next to the cargo hold of the aircraft, the tug with Sean's shipping container pulled up. Once again I inspected the tug, cut the ties off the netting and validated that no tampering had taken place. I then entered the cargo area of the aircraft and checked it for hazards that could cause damage to the cargo. None seemed to exist, so I gave the order to load him. Once he was loaded, I checked the tie down straps and rechecked the paperwork on the shipping container just to make sure. Everything checked out and I boarded the plane. I found my seat and settled in for a flight to Atlanta. This was odd as we were traveling from Arizona to California but had a long layover in Atlanta. Apparently this was the only route available for the short turn around requested with this type of cargo. It was a two-hour flight filled with anxiety and the occasional passerby that would stop and thank me for my service. I have always appreciated this gesture, but I really never know what to say in response. I mean, do I thank them for thanking me or do I just say, *"you're welcome?"* At any rate, it's always very humbling.

We landed in Atlanta and I was let off the plane first and met plane-side with another luggage tug. This one had been specially retrofitted for caskets and had been painted with an American flag with the words "Never Forget" emblazoned on the side. I oversaw the loading and we drove to the nearest cargo hanger. The layover was several hours long, so I opted to stay in the cargo area near Sean's remains. Everyone was very accommodating. Airline employees brought me food and opened up the bay door so that I could smoke and still be in eye-shot of the casket. The time came to take off again and we traveled to the new aircraft. This time the pilot met me plane-side. He shook my hand and told me he had secured me a seat in first class. I declined, but he insisted telling me that all the other seats had been taken and I no longer had an option. He shared his appreciation for my service and told me not to hesitate to ask if I needed anything. He reported to the cockpit while I inspected the cargo area and watched the baggage team load the casket one last time. I then entered the plane and took my seat in first class.

Soon we were in the air again, the last leg on Sean's journey home. I must have fallen asleep from pure exhaustion because the next thing I remember is the pilot on the intercom announcing our arrival at Los Angeles International Airport. We touched down and as we taxied to the gate, the pilot came across the intercom again and said, "Ladies and Gentlemen, I've had the distinct honor to transport one of America's fallen soldiers home today. Please, do not be alarmed as the LAX Fire Department renders water salute over our aircraft as a sign of respect for our nation's hero. Also, please allow our uniformed service member to deplane so he may continue with the duty of escorting him home." The intercom went silent for what seemed like minutes, but it sounded as if the microphone was still keyed. Then out of the blue the pilot said in a somber tone "God Bless America."

I received several pats on the backs and handshakes as I left the aircraft. I took the stairs down and went plane-side; I noticed the LAX Honor Guard and the local Los Angeles Air Station Honor Guard team had assembled to present honors. I climbed up in the cargo area and oversaw the unstrapping and then removed the shipping container exposing the flag draped coffin. We loaded it onto the conveyor belt and I took my place next to the plane. The cargo belt started to move and the casket was suddenly visible to all. In the back ground "Taps" played and we all saluted. Once the casket was near the ground, the honor guard stepped up and loaded it into the hearse awaiting its arrival. I gave the order of *"dismissed"* and everyone started to leave. I looked up into the terminal and saw that a crowd had assembled at the windows and had been watching us in this moment of sorrow. In the middle of the crowd was a small boy holding tightly to his father's hand. Our eyes locked and what happened next brought a tear to my eye. He rendered me a salute. I had never been prouder to return a salute than I was at that moment. It made my pride swell and made me wonder about his future all in the same instant. I quickly jumped into the hearse and we were off to the funeral home.

We arrived a short time later and moved Sean's casket into the prep room. I removed the flag from the casket, unlocked it and opened the lid to check if he had shifted during the trip. What I saw surprised me. His makeup had dehydrated and his face was a bright pink. It was almost like someone has smeared Pepto-Bismol® all over his face. I was horrified! I did not know what to do. Then, I re-membered that my Funeral Director had given me her cell phone. *"And I thought I would never have a need to use it."* I thought to myself. I called the number in a panic; I explained the situation to her. She, as always, was calm and told me that she would handle it. She used her contacts in the area to locate a makeup artist to come in and correct the situation. I was relieved and now only had to secure my rental car for the next day and check into my hotel.

Once the makeup artist arrived, I went to the car rental place and was given the only car left on the lot, a pink hued PT Cruiser. This was quite a knock to my ego but I was so exhausted, I did not care. I left the lot and followed the GPS directions to my hotel. Imagine me driving in dress blues in a pink PT Cruiser in rush hour traffic. The GPS told me to take the next exit, so I did, and much to my dismay, found myself on Compton Ave. So now, I'm not only in a pink PT Cruiser, in dress blues but I'm on Compton Ave, a street notorious in the 80's and 90's rap songs I had been so fond of in my youth. Needless to say, I was scared out of my head. I finally arrived safely at my hotel and received a call from the makeup artist. She was finished and wanted me to check out her work so she could be paid and released. I met her at the chapel and discovered that she had come through with flying colors. The makeup was flawless. I paid her with my government purchase card and sent her on her way. I now could get some much-needed rest before the next day's service and funeral.

The next morning came way too fast. The services started at 9 am and I had crawled out of bed at 5 am so I could get breakfast, get dressed and still have time to arrive at the chapel a couple of hours early to meet with the family prior to the service. I went down to the courtyard restaurant and had a good breakfast, as it promised to be a long day full of uncertainty. I then went back to my room, showered, put on my service dress uniform once again and headed out. As I pulled into the parking lot, I searched for the furthest parking spot away from the entrance to hide my rental car and went into the chapel. I was greeted by the director of services and we checked the remains one last time. The makeup had held up overnight so I wheeled his casket into the chapel and centered it in front of the pulpit. I repositioned the flag over the casket and opened it in preparation for the family viewing and service. Just as I had finished I was startled by a loud painful scream, "NO!" someone cried from the front of the chapel. It was Sean's sister standing in the doorway sobbing in disbelief. Her brother was dead and she was not ready to accept this fact.

Her father moved over to her to console her, the entire family entered the chapel all sobbing and trying to be present for one another. I met them half way up the aisle, offering my hand for comfort. The father looked me in the eyes and through his tears I saw his gratitude. He said, "Thank you, sir." I nodded but did not speak, as I had no words that could alleviate their pain. They all moved to Sean's side and took turns with his remains, caressing his uniform and hands. They all stood in a line and asked if I would take pictures of them with the casket. I was taken aback. I had never heard of anyone wanting pictures with a corpse. But this was their way and who was I to judge? I obliged and snapped an endless amount of photos.

The father had asked me to hand out the funeral pamphlets they had printed to the guests that would be paying their respects. I positioned myself at the entrance to the chapel with a handful of these pamphlets and started handing them out to the guests that were now starting to arrive. There were a lot of people in attendance. Some were dressed in church clothes; others were wearing white t-shirts emblazoned with an airbrush painting of Sean with the Letters RIP in the center and on the rear. I later found out that these were members of Sean's former gang. Once the service started, I shut the doors to the chapel and excused myself out back to have a cigarette. While I was smoking, a man in his mid-forties came out back wearing one of these t-shirts. He looked at me and said, "Are you the guy that brought Sean home?" I nodded and he moved in very close to me. A tear fell from his cheek and he whispered in my ear, "Thank you for taking care of him." I simply looked at him and nodded in a somber manner. He lit up his own cigarette and turned to me and said, "I like your colors." I asked him, *"My what?"* To which he responded, "Your colors, you know... ribbons." I looked down at my chest full of ribbons and decorations and said, *"Oh, thanks, man."* He wanted to know what each one of them was for, so I spent the next few minutes explaining each one to him. We finished our break and as we headed back inside he invited me to a party that they were having in Sean's honor that night. I politely declined telling him I had a plane to catch late that evening and we parted ways.

The service completed and the father asked me to move his son into the back to prepare him for transport to the cemetery. We had about thirty minutes so I moved him into the preparatory room, closed his casket and locked it. Then, I draped the flag again and turned to leave the room. As my hand grabbed the door handle, I noticed it was very cold to the touch. I heard something move behind me. I turned to look and just behind the casket I saw what appeared to be an apparition standing behind the casket. I was startled and rubbed my eyes to make sure I wasn't seeing things. I looked closer and I could vaguely see it was Sean standing there looking at me. This scared the shit out of me, but then this apparition did something that made it all okay, at least in my mind. It gave me a thumbs up. Some of you may be thinking I'm crazy at this point and I am sure this was all generated in my mind, but it helped me that day, it really did. We loaded up the casket in the hearse and took down the curtains so that everyone could see the flag draped casket as the procession headed to the cemetery. Along the way people were lining the streets with flags and some holding hands. Though he had not died in battle he still died serving his country and his neighbors welcomed him home in the only way they knew how.

We arrived at the cemetery and I exited the hearse to help guide the driver to the area where the casket was to be unloaded by the honor guard. While the team members unloaded the casket, I met with the team lead and gave him instructions on who the mother and father were so he knew who to offer the folded flag to. I met with the father and told him where I would be. He shook my hand and went to his seat. I moved to the rear of the crowd as the funeral began. The preacher said a few words, the family released doves, "Taps" was played, followed by a 21 gun salute, and the honor guard team lead offered the mother the flag that had been laid on her son's casket and said, "Ma'am, please accept this on behalf of a grateful nation."

Needless to say, I was choked up, but the time had come to move Sean's casket into the family's mausoleum to its final resting place. Out of the corner of my eye I saw the father waving to me to come to him. I moved quickly to him and he asked that I escort his son into the crypt. I agreed but had not planned on this so I improvised. I placed my right hand on the casket took my position on Sean's left as the position to the right is always reserved as a position of honor. I walked slowly at pace as the cemetery staff wheeled him down a long hallway to his crypt. They knelt down, opened his crypt and placed the casket inside and then closed it forever. I rendered one last slow and solemn salute to Sean and then turned to leave. As I looked up the hall of the mausoleum packed with family and friends, there was not a dry eye in the place. My mission was complete. My time with A1C Sean Campos was done. Although I never met him while he was alive, I will always know him in spirit, and carry with me the pain of his family's loss.

Photo a derivative of *Taps Bugler* © 2009 DoD Mass Communication Specialist 1st Class Chad J. McNeeley

CHAPTER 10
Al Udied, Deployment 4

When I stepped off the plane onto the airfield at Al Udied Air Base, Qatar, my initial impression was typical, excruciatingly hot and dusty, a scene I was all too familiar with from my other three tours in the region. The base was bigger than any other I had deployed to in the past, but it had the same run down feel to it. As I crossed the tarmac, I noticed waves of heat coming off the concrete and thought to myself, *"Here we go again."* But this time it was different. I had been assigned as the team lead, a vested E-6 who had been in the military for over fifteen years and now I was not just responsible for myself, but the welfare of my entire team as well. My team consisted of 18 individuals and half of them had arrived in country two weeks prior and were already hard at work.

My first order of business was to get everyone to their living quarters (hooches) and then go visit my advance team members. One in particular I was eager to see, a subordinate of mine from home station in Arizona, SSgt Starnes. He had told me in email communications that he had been assigned as the Readiness and Mortuary NCO for the deployment and I wanted to make damn sure he had a good handle on his tasks. I walked into his work center and we met at the door. He seemed rushed and gave me a surprised "Hey Sarge." greeting. I shook his hand as he told me that he was on his way to the airfield to receive some HRs. (HR stands for human remains. When a service member or a contractor dies while in the theater of war, their remains are sent to evacuation points and prepared for shipment home.) He asked if I'd like to join him. I sensed he was eager to show me how well he did his job, so I agreed. We piled into his truck and headed out to the flight line to meet with the Aircraft Commander. On the way, we discussed his time on deployment thus far, and he helped me get familiar with the base by pointing out some landmarks. He also prepared me for the mission we were about to accomplish and what actions he had taken to ensure smooth dignified transfers.

After an arduous drive through different security checkpoints and over unpaved roads abuzz with the business of warfighter support, we arrived at the airfield and met with the volunteer-based dignified transfer team. A four member team comprised of Airman and NCOs from different functional areas of the base, most had done this before, with the large number of transfers this base did and SSgt Starnes had trained them all very well. He got out of the truck, introduced us to each member of the team and gave detailed directions on how to properly off load and transfer the remains into his truck, a covered vehicle that resembled a bread truck. SSgt Starnes then gave everyone an opportunity to back out of this detail. We always take great care to ensure that our volunteers have a solid grasp on what they were going to encounter. No one backed out. SSgt Starnes was insistent that I just stand by and watch, but I would have none of that. I'm a hand's on type of guy so I told him, *"You may be the one in charge here, but I'm still the boss. Let's do this."* Our drive up to the aircraft was less than 500 feet but the mandatory 5 mph speed limit made it seem like forever. We finally pulled up to the aircraft and I jumped out of the van to spot SSgt Starnes towards the rear getting as close as possible and still allowing us to remove the remains. Great caution must be taken while performing this duty but you want to draw the least amount of attention possible, because just seeing a flag draped casket can cause those working in the area serious distress. On this day, there were four transfer cases. We met with the Loadmaster and the Aircraft Commander to develop a plan for removing the remains and transporting them to our mortuary cooler. Once a plan was agreed upon, our team positioned themselves around the first transfer case and awaited SSgt Starnes's commands: "Detail... attention!" "Ready... lift!" "Detail, forward march!"

As we made our way down the aircraft ramp carrying someone's deceased son, daughter, father or mother, my mind raced with a single thought, *"Don't drop it. Don't drop it."* After years in the mortuary services, I find that I have a tendency to fixate on the worst-case scenario. In spite of the fact that I knew deep down I would never allow myself to drop a transfer case, at that moment it was THE worst thing that could happen. Looking back, I think my ability to fixate kept me from being complacent in my duties. Therefore, it ended up being a good thing, I guess.

Thankfully, the off-loading and transfer to cold storage went according to plan. We thanked the dignified transfer team for their help and then dismissed them. At that point, SSgt Starnes looked at me and said, "What'd ya think?" I gave him kudos but, being in the business for as long as I had, I knew that the job was only half done. We entered the cooler, removed the flags from the transfer cases, stowed them properly and unlatched the sides of the transfer cases to expose the body bags contained in each. We checked the identification tags to see if they were legible enough for the medical examiners at the Port Mortuary in Dover AFB to read and then we drained the ice and fluids that had accumulated in the cases in flight.

There are no drainage spouts on transfer cases. So, to effectively drain a case requires two people, one person to lift the case at the head and another to secure the body bag inside so it wouldn't fall out. The second man's job is accomplished by placing their hands on the center of the body bag and as the case is lifted positioning their shoulder center mass on the bag. The problem is, one can never be certain which end is the head without feeling around on the body bag to find it.

On this particular day, I was the one securing the body bags. We got through the first two cases without too much issue. However, as we drained the cases my boots and pant legs became covered in bloody water. I selfishly thought, *"Oh great! Those are totally ruined!"* I'm handling a dead hero and all I can think about is ruining my boots. This still troubles me today, I have become very good at self-loathing.

On the third case, there was a problem. As I went to secure the body against my shoulder, SSgt Starnes began the lift and the body bag collapsed over my shoulder. I struggled to regain control of the bag but up until that moment I hadn't considered that the bags may be filled with not only bodies but parts of bodies. The fragmented remains tumbled inside of the bag collecting in the bottom near the zipper area which was resting near the middle of my back. Suddenly, I felt a rush of cold liquid flowing down my back and onto my legs. The horror I felt is indescribable. It wasn't the idea of the blood or the sheer gore of the situation that bothered me, but my negligent assumption that all remains were going to be intact. That, and the fact that my subordinate had just witnessed the consequence of my incorrect assumption. I regained my composure and I am not even sure he saw what had happened, being positioned behind the transfer case, nevertheless, it bothered me. We had one more HR to complete, and this time I took great care not to repeat the incident.

That was the day that the war became real to me. To this day, every time I see a cup of ice, I'm taken back. I can see the bloody ice no matter how hard I try to block it out. I still have frequent dreams of standing in knee deep bloody ice. Afterward, I would sit in my room at night and I could see the terrified agony on the faces of my brothers and sisters in arms, dying on the battlefield. Legs blown off, eyes gone, faces burnt and smashed, never to return to their families alive again. I began to obsess, *"Why them and not me?"* I felt so badly about previously lobbying my leadership at home base to get SSgt Starnes assigned to my work center. He had proven his worth in every section he had been assigned to and I wanted to get him assigned to my shop, because I wanted the best. I always tried to surround myself with the best people and SSgt Starnes was definitely that. From then on in the deployment I went on as many transfers as I could with SSgt Starnes. I saw it as playing kind of a protective father role, even though he was more than capable. An idea he wasn't thrilled about.

It seemed like we would have at least one transfer every day and most days mutable HRs at the same time. I would silently check every bag tag to make sure it wasn't one of my friends down range. At night, I would feel guilty for feeling relief that it wasn't one of my friends. As if a perfect stranger's death was less important to me. The truth of the matter is, I cared, and I cared deeply for everyone who had fallen, even those I did not know. I treated all remains as if they were family members, with dignity and respect. In retrospect, that may have been a mistake because I have buried hundreds of heroes over the years and it has taken a toll on my mind.

As the deployment went on, I began to settle more into my primary role as the second in charge of the largest ration warehouse in the Air Force. We handled the delivery and issue of food for the nearly 10,000 troops stationed at Al Udied. I was surrounded by the constant buzz of forklifts and tractor-trailers coming in and out of the warehouse area. I was in charge of day to day operations on the floor in two sections, dry storage and cold storage. We resupplied several dining facilities on site storage locations daily. The days were long and hard and it seemed like we were always running into some type of problem with equipment or on time deliveries. One day, towards the end of my deployment, one of the third country national contractors came to me and said that other contractors were stealing from us. He would not tell me who, just that it was happening. It made sense. Our accounting numbers were off by thousands of dollars every month. I had assumed that my staff was being lazy and miscounting during inventories. I got in their ass for this, but they all swore it didn't have anything to do with them. This information gave me all the excuse I needed to start watching everyone like a hawk.

It didn't take long and one day I noticed something odd. Three contractors were emptying the trash with a forklift. I thought to myself, "Why wouldn't they just load the trash into provided trash carts and then wheel it out to the dumpster?" I walked toward them as they hurried to unload the trash and then took off quickly. I found their behavior odd because they were usually very cordial. We had had many conversations in the last few months and never had they scampered away from me. I looked into the dumpster and saw it loaded with black trash bags. Certainly that was nothing out of the ordinary but then I noticed the bags were wet. I felt the bag that was located near the top of the heap and it was freezing cold. I removed my knife from my belt, cut open the bag and I was floored! It was full of frozen pork products, ribs, bacon, diced pork…you name it, it was there. The dumpster was full from bottom to the top with these bags. There must have been fifteen bags or more.

© Justin Jordan

I went directly into the kitchen area and alerted the superintendent and she immediately called the police. She told me later that she had suspected they were stealing pork and selling it on the black market, she just didn't know how. The police arrived and emptied the dumpster. They opened every bag spread it out over the rocks and took account of all the frozen pork products. Almost $7500 worth! The three contractors were arrested, questioned and handed over to the Qatari Government Police.

The investigators also interviewed me,

© Justin Jordan

took my statement, and explained that the contractors were coordinating their abuse with the garbage collection service driver and this was only one of the locations they were hitting. The Driver would sell the pork, a black market commodity in Muslim countries, for triple the cost and share the profits with the contractors. Once the dust settled, I found out that this had been going on for nearly a year and they had made off with nearly 1.5 million dollars in pork products. Everyone in senior leadership patted me on the back for uncovering the fraud. Awards were handed out and the base General even gave me his coveted coin for excellence. During the course of the next few weeks, I often wondered what happened to those three contractors. I asked one of the other contractors who lived with them off base. He told me they were executed. I was instantly sick. I was horrified; I told myself it could not be true. I went straight to the investigator and asked him the same question. He confirmed my fears. I was responsible for the death of three men. Yes, they were stealing. But did they deserve to die for it? They were just trying to feed their families. I was having a hard time shaking this one off. It tore at my core. I think my leadership noticed my change in demeanor because they moved me to a different section shortly thereafter. It was a welcome change, but I still spent the last few weeks of my deployment walking around in a daze. I still have dreams about those three contractors. I feel responsible for their deaths and do not know if I can ever forgive myself for doing the

"Right Thing."

Years later when I told this story in a therapy group, a war hardened, combat vet across the room from me tried to interject some levity by saying "Great! I have been deployed six times, saw my fair share of conflict and now I hear a fucking cook got three KIAs? That's just great!" We all laughed but it wasn't really funny. He was merely trying to alleviate some of my guilt. I often wonder about the families of those three contractors. If they knew what I had done, would they want me dead? I may never know. The one thing I do know is they did not deserve to die regardless of whether it was the right thing to do or not.

CHAPTER 11
The Lost Suicide

I arrived home from a long day of wartime exercise planning meetings and training. These types of days always mentally exhausted me. I saw my wife sitting out on the back porch watching T.V. I settled into the chair next to her in hopes of discussing our day as we had a thousand times before. She told me one of her co-workers was called back from deployment early because of family problems. No one has seen him in two days and she was concerned. The word going around the squadron was that his wife had met someone while he was deployed and that left him to move in with the new guy. He had last been seen at his estranged wife's place of employment carrying a gun. Then he disappeared. I didn't give it much thought as these types of things happen quite often while husbands and wives are deployed. The part about the gun did strike me as odd. Maybe he went there to scare her, thought better of it and left. We continued to discuss our days for the next few hours and watched our favorite T.V. shows before my wife decided to go to bed. I stayed up to chat with my neighbor, Larry.

The next morning, I mentioned what my wife had said to one of my subordinates. She asked me if I thought he might have killed himself. The thought had not crossed my mind but I got agitated and I snapped at her, *"Why would he do that? That's such a pussy move!"* I was still feeling the pain of the last suicide I had worked, but there was no getting around it. The seed had been planted in my mind. Days went by and word circulated on base that there was a search party looking for the missing Airman. Base helicopters were being used to assist the local authorities in the search. My wife and I frequently discussed the local gossip but, no one seemed to know what had happened to him.

A few weeks went by. Most had forgotten he was missing. One afternoon, I was walking out the door to head to lunch when my cell phone rang. It was the command post. They had found him dead in a local construction yard by an apparent self-inflicted gunshot wound to the head. My heart sunk. I was livid at him for doing this! *How could he put us all through this?* To this day, the mere thought of suicide drives me to a white-knuckle rage. I get so mad that someone could be that selfish. I went back into the office and started the paperwork. Once there, I received a call from the Funeral Director. She had already received the remains. This was odd. I had not spoken to the family yet and the authorities had only just found him before this call. The Funeral Director said she was puzzled too. She stated that no autopsy had been performed. I told her I would track down some more information and get back to her.

I immediately went to the Commander's office to brief him. He was not available so I headed back to my office to call the coroner and asked why an autopsy had not been performed. Typical with most government offices, I was transferred several times before being able speak to someone who had some insight on the issue. The pathologist assigned to our case determined the cause of death to be an apparent suicide and, as such, determined that an autopsy was not necessary. I explained to him that federal government policy mandated that autopsies be performed in all active duty deaths regardless of circumstance. He became short with me, stated that he did not work for the federal government and then hung up on me. I thought to myself, *"Great! What am I going to do now?"* But the good thing about working at the federal level is that there was always someone to call to help you enforce the standards.

Finally, I got in touch with the Commander and briefed him on the situation. He made a few calls and then, low and behold, our deceased service member was on his way to the coroner's office for autopsy. It had been a long day and I was on my way home when my cell rang again. It was the Funeral Director again, she sounded shaken. I asked her what was going on and she said, "I just had to let you know, this guy was infested." I responded with, *"Infested?"* She went on to explain that he had been out in the desert so long that he was infested head to toe with insects, primarily maggots. The thought nauseated me. She continued to explain the importance of suggesting cremation to the family when we met because no airline would let him fly with an insect infestation.

I arrived home and decided I'd keep this nugget of news to myself since my wife had worked with him. I feared it may be too much for her to handle. So I went to bed wondering what my next days had in store for me, imagining the worst. I didn't sleep at all that night. Not that I wasn't tired, I was scared of the dreams I knew I would have. The next day I arrived at work exhausted and uneasy about what I was to see that day. First thing that morning, the Commander called me into his office. He told me that due to the decomposed state of the remains he had concerns about me attending the inspection that afternoon. He told me he would handle it and that I need not to worry about it. At first, I was relieved. I had already spent the whole night obsessing about what I was going to see and what the remains would look like. I could not escape my thoughts.

I went back to my office and tried to focus on the other aspects of my duties. The more I tried the harder it became to push the thoughts out of mind. I decided that I had to see him, if only to alleviate the thoughts. Maybe it wouldn't be that bad. Maybe it would settle the images I had conjured. Now that I had decided that I was going to see the remains, I had to figure out how I was going to do this without the Commander knowing. This went against my better judgment as I was, in essence, disobeying a direct order and could be risking my career. But I had made up my mind. Now I had to figure out how to put my plan in motion. As the day went on the Commander informed me that we had to meet with the estranged wife, since she was still listed as his next of kin. This promised to be a tense meeting because the parents of the deceased also planned on attending. I could only imagine the emotion that would hang heavy in this room.

As all of this was going on I received a call from the coroner's office. The autopsy was complete and they wanted to know where to transport the remains, this meant I had to consult with the family. But which side should I consult? The parents, or the estranged wife? I contacted my headquarters to get some guidance. They informed me that the wife had the legal right to direct disposition of his remains, regardless of circumstance, since they were still legally married. To this end, I made contact with the wife. Thankfully, she decided that she would consult with her husband's family and get back to me on which funeral home to send him to. Ten minutes later, she called back and told me to use the contract funeral home we typically used. I called the coroner's office and gave them the information. They agreed to transport him later that day. The Commander had set up the family briefing for the next day. The parents of the deceased were en route to our location and the wife felt it important that they be a part of the meeting. That afternoon, during my commute home, I experienced my first dissociative episode.

I have no recollection of how I got there but, I ended up in Phoenix almost two hours away from my home. I was alone and scared and had no idea how I had gotten there. It was puzzling and frightening all at once. The only reason I knew I was in Phoenix was the traffic signs. I turned the car around and headed home. I knew no one would miss me because of the late hours I typically kept during an active case. It was a long ride home and I was still fighting the images that cropped up in my mind. The only way I could calm myself was to listen to my favorite talk radio host on satellite radio. He made me laugh and kept my mind occupied long enough to get me home. I don't have clear memories of that night but I do remember waking up with no voice again. Luckily, the Commander did the majority of the speaking during our meetings with the families. I spent a good portion of the morning drinking tea, sucking on lozenges, and eventually gained my voice back by mid-day.

The time had come to meet with the family. We entered the home and introduced ourselves. You could have cut the tension in the room with a knife. The wife was sitting at the table in the center of the room just off the kitchen. The decedent's parents and another person I assumed was a sibling were huddled in the kitchen, whispering and watching with crossed arms. The Commander sat at the table and started his briefing with the wife. She didn't say much until the discussion about cremation came up. She looked at the family in the kitchen, as if to get their approval. They stated that due to religious beliefs they were against cremation. She declined the option. At this point I could no longer hold my tongue, I explained to them that the condition of the remains made it impossible to fly him home for burial. They were insistent and began lobbing insults at us, something about how the government was able to put a man on the moon but, they couldn't get their dead son home. I tried to explain federal guidelines about transporting remains with infestations to them, but they would not hear of it.

At that point, the Commander chimed in. He assured them we would do what we could and get back to them. When we left, the Commander told me to get with the funeral home and discuss other options. I decided I would just drive to the funeral home and meet with them. This was also my chance to see the remains and put my visions to rest. I entered the funeral home and it was empty. There was a sign saying they were out at a function and to call a number they had posted if you needed immediate assistance. I looked around to ensure no one was there and I proceeded to the back. I entered the room and the smell had a chemical aroma. Then I saw him. I knew who I was looking for because I had met him once or twice. I moved to his side. He had a large hole in the left side of his head. His body was gray and stiff. As I looked closer, I could see the maggots eating his flesh. Some of his skin was moving slightly from the insects inside and he had a grim look in his eyes.

I ran as fast as I could out of there. The sight of him was much more gruesome than I had imagined. I immediately questioned my rationale. The images I had now were much worse than before. *"What have I done?"* I drove straight home and called my Commander. I told him I was feeling ill and requested the rest of the day off. He agreed because he knew I was struggling with laryngitis that morning. I arrived to an empty house. I sat on the back porch and for the first time I contemplated ending my life. The thought quickly faded, as I had seen firsthand the devastation suicide caused. Who would watch my son graduate? Who would walk my baby girl down the aisle? At that moment I decided I am not going to let these mother fucking thoughts beat me. I was going to fight it and I was going to win. I went to my room, my head pounding with pain and fell asleep until the next morning. No dreams. No visions. Just rest.

I was awakened by my cell phone ringing the next morning. It was the Funeral Director apologizing for missing my call. We discussed the family meeting. She offered up a solution. A Ziegler case is a hermetically sealed metal case that fits into the casket. This was the only way airlines would accept infested remains. I was relieved but needed to get approval due to the cost associated with the product. I called the mortuary headquarters and explained the situation. They would not approve the use of a Ziegler Case. They felt that enough had not been done to properly rid the remains of its infestation. Besides, there was no precedent. I briefed the Commander on the situation and he asked to call the Funeral Director and put her on speaker phone in his office. She explained that she had gone to extraordinary lengths to rid him of these infestations, even dipping the remains in kerosene to try and kill the bugs. Now I knew what the chemical smell was when I entered the back room at the funeral home. The Commander worked a deal with her to give us the Ziegler case at cost and he would pay for the rest out of his discretionary funds.

I left the Commander's office and started preparing the decedent's uniform. The family had requested I purchase a brand new set of dress blues so I had to get them tailored in a hurry. I dropped them off at the tailor, gave them instructions and told them I would be back the next morning to pick them up. I arrived home that night and discussed my worries about his uniform not fitting him with my wife. She offered to stop by my office and try it on as they were about the same height. I agreed thinking nothing of it at the time. The next morning, I picked up the uniform and ribbon rack. My wife arrived and put on the uniform. As I placed the ribbons on her chest, we locked eyes. At that moment, I saw a flash of her on the mortician's table, dead, decayed with a fearful look in her eyes. It scared the shit out of me! I must have gasped because she asked me, "What's wrong?" I shrugged it off and rushed her out of the room. Overwhelmed with anxiety and guilt, I sat there at my desk trying not to sob.

For a long time after that I could not look into my wife's eyes for fear that the flashing image would return. I delivered the uniform to the funeral home and, since he would be in a Ziegler case, told them there was no need for further inspection of the remains. As far as I was concerned I was done with this case except for the paperwork and the calls to the receiving funeral home. But, make no mistake this case had changed me forever. It cut me to my core. I saw behind the curtain of humanity and did not like what I saw. My family and friends started to notice changes in me and asked that I seek help. I started contemplating the idea and would even drive by the mental health clinic, sometimes even stopping and eating my lunch in the parking lot hoping to muster up the courage to go in and say, *"Help me, please!"* I was scared. Scared of the stigmas associated with getting mental health assistance, scared of what others would think of me and worst of all, scared of admitting defeat. This case started out with trying to find a missing Airman and somewhere along the way I was the one who got lost. I was now in an unfamiliar world. Everything frightened me, I was no longer the great Sergeant Jordan. Now, I was just a guy that would someday die. I have often wondered if, in his haste to end his life, the decedent in this case had contemplated the effect that his passing would have on others. You may have noticed I used no name, not even a made up one while telling this story. My feelings towards him are sharp and jagged. I have nothing but disdain for him. If I could tell him one thing, I would say… **"FUCK YOU. Just FUCK YOU!"**

CHAPTER 12
Why Didn't Daddy Love Me? (A Dream)

It always starts the same way on a particularly gloomy day in the middle of the monsoon season in Arizona. The rain fell like heavy balls of warm lead that hit you in the face with unrelenting force. I was outside smoking, taking shelter under a tree near the designated smoking area when the call came in. I quickly extinguished my cigarette and ran inside to field the call. I didn't quite make it before the phone went to voicemail. I decided to head upstairs to my office before listening to the voicemail. I needed to get prepared to take down the information I needed.

I listened to the voicemail. It was the command post with a mortuary notification. I called the number and the technician on the other end stated that there had been an active duty suicide by hanging in a residence on base. I started gathering my paperwork and prepared to brief the Commander. Because this happened on base we arranged for the family to house in our temporary lodging facilities typically used for families transferring into base. I arranged for the Commander to meet with the family and I called the coroner to pick up the body for autopsy. Then I hustled over to the gate to escort the coroner onto the base and took them over to the residence by way of back roads and side streets to avert attention and avoid as much collateral distress as possible.

We arrived at the home and introduced ourselves to the Security Forces personnel staged at the door processing the scene. The man from the coroner's office was a young guy in his early twenties working his way through college. He had an upbeat demeanor which troubled me so I asked him, *"Why are you so upbeat? There's a dead guy in there."* He looked back and chuckled, "If I don't stay upbeat I'll end up like you, all sad and withered." I twisted my face in disapproval and before I could fire back he interrupted, "Settle down, big guy. I was joking. "I do this shit all day long and use humor as my defense." Begrudgingly I nodded, because I kind of understood his point. He then asked me, "What is the scene like?" I told him, *"He hung himself, but I haven't been in yet."* We entered the house and were led to the back bedroom and there he was still hanging from a board he had screwed into the ceiling just off center. It appeared he did this so he could step off the bed to complete the task. I turned to leave and the young man asked me, "Where are you going?" I looked at him puzzled. "You have to hold him while I cut him down," he demanded. I must have looked mortified because he said "I can always get one of the cops to do it, but they usually fumble things up." I sighed and put on a protective suit he had brought in with him. The young man set up his gurney, got a ladder and positioned himself near the top with a knife ready to cut the rope. I positioned myself near the hips of the deceased, placing my arms under his rear end and on the coroner's assistant order I lifted. He made very quick work of the rope and the body fell collapsing on to my shoulder. The body was stiff and rigid and I didn't quite know what to do next. I thought to myself, *"Should I just stand there with this dead guy in my arms?"* I decided to lay him down on the gurney as delicately as I could, which caused the coroner assistant to comment, "You're not going to hurt him, he's dead." I just shook my head and headed outside to take the bunny suit off. I felt as though I may vomit.

The coroner's assistant came out a short time later with the gurney. I helped him load the remains into his van and he drove off base. I spent the next few hours filling out paperwork and reflecting on the day's events. Very little surprised me anymore, but I couldn't shake the *"did that really just happen?"* feeling. When I arrived home that night, I was disappointed; Larry was nowhere to be found. His house was dark and no cars were in the driveway. At first, I was pissed. *"How dare he not be there for me."* But after a few beers I noticed a light go on in his house, heard his sliding glass door open, and the sound of him lighting his cigarette. I popped my head up and said, *"Hey man! Where ya been?"* He explained that his wife had made him take her out to dinner with their three kids and he was glad to finally be home. We spent a long time just shooting the shit and drinking beer. Looking back now, I wonder if he understands how much he helped me through some of the hardest times in my life.

The next day we met with the family to go over arrangements. I decided to fade into the backdrop on this briefing, because I was still quite taken by the events of the day prior. I stood just out of sight from the table, but close enough to hear if the Commander or the wife had any questions. I felt outside of my head, in a far off place and yet I was still cognizant of what was going on. I caught myself thinking about being out on the Gulf of Mexico fishing with my best friend, Derek. Those are some of my fondest memories, just two guys, no phones and plenty of beer. I was brought back to reality when the wife started sobbing, cussing, and screaming at her deceased husband, "Why you mother-fucker? Why would you leave me?" I stepped around the corner to see if I could aide in any way. I noticed a doorway down the hall open slightly and a small girl, maybe six or seven years old, poked her head out. She noticed me and ducked back in quickly. I thought nothing of it and offered the wife a tissue. She knocked it out of my hand and said, "You know what? Burn that motherfucker! Cremate his ass!" I stepped back, picked up the tissue and laid it on the table next to her then resumed my post around the corner. I continued to see the door pop open and close quickly down the hall, almost like the little girl was playing peek a boo. I could tell she was scared, upset and just want to go to her Mom. But some-thing was obviously stopping her. After the meeting was finished, I couldn't help but wonder if that something that stopped her was me? I felt terrible. What if my presence was preventing the little girl from trying to console her mother? I tried to dismiss the notion but sometimes I still wonder.

I went back to the office and started arranging transport and inspections of the remains with our funeral home. It was troubling to me how efficient I had become at such a morbid series of tasks. But, in the end, I tried to accept that this was my job and I had become very good at it. The Funeral Director and I decided that the next day would be best for the inspections. I briefed this to the Commander and he asked if I could handle this one on my own. This was not something that was typically done but I agreed. I went home that day and sat in solitude on the back porch. I needed to be alone with my thoughts. I was strug-gling with what I had seen in the previous days and I had begun to suffer from the increase in anxiety. I smoked a lot that night and drank many beers. Eventu-ally, I passed out. The next morning I awoke still sitting in the chair. I went into the house and saw my wife getting ready for work. She asked if I was just getting home, because I was still in uniform. I lied and told her yes. I just could not share this one with her. I was starting to fear that if I shared the truth with her it may affect her in a way I wasn't prepared to accept responsibility for. I moved past her and got into the hottest shower I could stand. Today promised to bring more of the same that the past two had, maybe worse.

I had gotten a pretty late start on the day, so I bypassed work and went straight to the funeral home. I arrived at the funeral home to the usual pleasantries and we retired to the prep room in the rear. When I saw him laid out on the stainless steel table I got angry. I thought to myself, *"What a bitch! What a selfish, son of a bitch! Didn't he realize the pain he caused, not only to his family but to his co-workers? To me?"* I wanted to punch him in his lifeless face. I wanted to scream. I made my recommendations to the Funeral Director and spoke to the wife about proceeding with the cremation. She mentioned that she would like to see him before the cremation took place. I strongly recommended that she reconsider, but her mind was made up. I notified the Funeral Director so they could apply makeup and make him presentable for her viewing. The Funeral Director told me this happened frequently in her line of work and it would be nothing she couldn't handle.

I arranged for the wife to meet me later that afternoon for her viewing. As the time drew near, the anxious feeling I had previously experienced began to overwhelm me. However, this time there was no beer to drink so I decided to ride it out in the parking lot with the aid of as many cigarettes as I could handle. I don't know why but smoking seemed to calm me down, something I still struggle with. At the allotted time I sprayed myself with cologne and went to the latrine in the funeral home to gargle with some mouthwash before entering the family conference room. This was an area that families would meet with the Funeral Directors to discuss arrangements and payment options. It was a large room with an ornate wooden conference table in the center. It had very comfortable leather bound chairs and the entire room had been framed in stained glass windows which gave it a church-like feel.

While I was setting up the room with water and tea for the arrival of the wife, the Funeral Director entered and told me she had just arrived and was waiting in the lobby. I walked down the hall to meet her and noticed that sitting with her was the same little girl I had seen briefly at the temporary lodging facility. I was confused and thought to myself, *"Why on earth would you allow your daughter to see this?"* I greeted them and led them to the conference room where we met with the Funeral Director and discussed what she would see in the next room. The little girl was less than interested in the conversation, as she was busy coloring in a book her mother had brought to occupy her. The wife explained that she needed to see him one last time and then asked if I could stay and watch her daughter while she went in. I scoffed at this, as typically I escorted the family members into this area. But, before I could even get any words out in protest the Funeral Director interrupted and said, "He normally escorts the family to the back. However, if you are comfortable with me going with you and Sergeant Jordan has no objections, I don't see a problem." I immediately agreed, but deep down I knew did not want to see his corpse again. I feared my anger would be apparent and possibly cause her more stress.

The wife left escorted by the Funeral Director and the room fell silent. The only sound was the crayons rubbing against the paper as the little girl scribbled in her book. I then asked her, "What are you coloring?" She stopped for a moment, looked up at me and did not say a word. She looked down again and started coloring, as if I hadn't said anything to her. I was kind of pissed but decided not to push the issue. Just then it happened. The visions, the memories all came flooding back. I started trying to breathe slowly as my palms grew sweaty and my knees started to shake. I thought to myself, *"No way can this happen now. Not now. Not here. I can't let this innocent child see me break down."* The sound of her little voice broke through my thoughts as she said to me, "Why didn't my daddy love me?"

Photo from the collection *"Free for All Creative Commons"* © 2009 D Sharon Pruitt, www.flickr.com/photos/pinksherbet

My mind went blank. I was truly at a loss for words. I struggled to formulate a response that would make her pain disappear. Just as I was about to speak the mother rushed into the room in tears, grabbed her daughter, and rushed out the door. Now, I was really angry at the deceased!!!! How could he be so self-centered? What a dirt bag! I wanted to fucking bring him back to life so I could kill him myself. I collected myself, arranged for the cremation, transport of the ashes to the family, and happily closed the book on this case. Since then, not a day has passed by when the little girl's voice hasn't resounded in my mind... *"Why didn't daddy love me?"* even if it was JUST a dream.

CHAPTER 13
That Day...That Day

I remember that day like one remembers their phone number. It takes little effort to mentally access it. Engraved in my subconscious, this day is an indelible part of who I am. I remember the sights, the sounds, the smells, and yet it was all a blur. I had just returned to the office from a trip around base, tightening up some training requirements for some of my subordinates working in different sections. We were discussing everyone's lunch plans and joking around. I was in a very jovial mood and had agreed to buy everyone in the office lunch, if they could beat me in a game of trash can basketball. We began the game, and as usual, I was scoring well and talking a lot of trash *(pun intended)*. Then the phone rang, not my mortuary cell but my office phone. I thought nothing of it and moved to my desk to answer it. I answered the phone with my typical protocol but with some laughter in my voice. *"Readiness, Plans and Mortuary, this is Sergeant Jordan. How may I help you?"* The phone was quiet but I could hear commotion in the background. I held up my hand to tell everyone in the office to be quiet. *"Readiness, Plans and Mortuary, this is Sergeant Jordan. How may I help you?"* I said again. A voice came over the line, "Hold on please." I stood by waiting, for what, I had no idea. I knew it could not be a mortuary case or they would have called my cell, so I was at a loss on what to think. The others all headed out to the smoking area to have a cigarette, giving me a gesture that looked like they were smoking so I would know where they were. I nodded and continued to hold. Two or three minutes go by and I say, *"Hello?"* The voice came back on, "Just a little longer, please." I started to get concerned, but had no idea why. I sat down at my desk, aggravated that someone called me and placed me on hold. Just then the voice came back on the line, "Is this the mortuary office?" I was confused but answered in turn, *"Yes it is, this is Sergeant Jordan, the NCOIC."* A small pause then, "I have a message to pass to you from the Incident Commander on scene at an accident on base." I gulped and said, *"Okay, go ahead."* I heard rustling paper in the background and he said, "Your presence has been requested at the parking lot near the Combined Air Operations Center.

We have two casualties, last name Biel, Bill and Crista Biel." My heart dropped. I got chills and was hot all at the same time. I choked out in response, *"Can you repeat those names?"* He replied, "Bill and Crista Biel" I hung the phone up. I didn't care if he was done. I fell back into my chair and my head fell into my hands. Bill and Crista Biel were friends of the family. They lived just blocks from our home and our kids played together often. I knew I had to act fast, so I started out the door calling my wife on the way to tell her the news so that she could be on standby to pick up their kids from school if necessary. She couldn't believe they were dead, nor could I. I did not have the information of what had happened but it was very unusual for me to be called to the scene of an accident. I must have worn my emotions on my face because when I stopped by the Commander's office to give him the information, the squadron Chief asked me what was wrong. I told him what I knew and he insisted on tagging along to the scene. To this day, I have no idea why he went along with me but he did.

We arrived at the scene in a very large parking lot with about 300 cars in it. In the very front of the lot there was a street that separated the lot from the buildings. Directly to our left were the flight line and the guest aircraft parking area. This is where other branches of service and foreign Air force pilots would park their jets if they were in town doing training. I parked the car and jumped out. As I approached the scene I saw a ton of people standing around. On the road separating the lot from the building, a large aircraft forklift was sitting in idle. The on scene Commander recognized my presence and began briefing me on the situation. It was Bill's birthday and Crista had stopped by to take him to lunch. As they stepped off the curb onto the street, a forklift hit them, running over Crista's leg and foot and crushing Bill underneath the giant machine. I interrupted, *"Sir, so Crista is fine?"* He nodded and said, "Yes, she is en route to the hospital. But, she lost consciousness and has no idea Bill is gone." He then asked me to survey the scene and to contact a coroner because we could not move the body out of the roadway without their consent. They had jurisdiction on base. I walked over to the cops guarding the scene, doing the investigation and told them what I had to do so they raised the yellow crime scene tape and allowed me in. As I rounded the forklift, I saw him. He was on the ground covered in a small yellow plastic cover about the size of an apron. Every time the wind blew by it would lift the apron up and you could see the body. I must have stood there for a while staring because one of the cops tapped me on the shoulder and asked if I was okay. I stooped down and checked under the forklift. It was covered with blood and particles of skin. I moved around to the rear and noticed a blood trail that made it look like Bill had been dragged. I followed it and in my estimation it was three car lengths in distance and, at the beginning of the drag trail, you could see a large splatter of blood. This must have been where his head came in contact with the ground after the initial impact. I immediately got on the phone with the coroner and asked for expedited recovery of remains. I was denied, the office only had one van and we were last in line on a very busy day. I then got on the phone with the base hotel and told them to bring me several bed sheets so I could cover Bill properly. I purposely avoided Bill's corpse. If I didn't look at it then it wasn't true, at least that was my rationale. But the sheets were coming, so I had to face it soon.

I left the area and briefed the on scene Commander about the delay and gave him the news that we couldn't move him. I then walked back to my truck and called my wife to let her know Crista was still alive. This was the longest walk in my life. It felt like I was walking in quick sand. I couldn't shake the helplessness I felt, I knew what I had to do and I wasn't ready, I wasn't ready to see his body. I was frozen with fear. I called my wife and she was her usual supportive self, offering whatever was needed in regard to the children, a sentiment that was the furthest thing from my mind. I was focused on the fear and now guilt was settling in as Bill and I had recently had a falling out. On my last deployment my son and his daughter were caught watching porn on the Internet. We chalked it up to kids being curious, but Bill was upset. I sent him an e-mail apologizing and ensuring him that this was a one-time thing and it would never happen again. That was our last communication. Since then, anytime we saw each other we simply gave a customary head nod and said not a word to each other. I thought to myself, *"Why didn't I try harder to mend this relationship? Why did I allow it to fester?"*

Just then the lodging employees arrived with my sheets. Once again, I made that devastatingly, long walk back to where Bill's body lay. I collected the sheets and carried them on to the scene. I stood over his body for a minute and then removed the covering, and there he was crushed, mangled, and bloodied with a blank stare in his eyes. I took a deep breath and began to cover his body. The sheets immediately turned red with his blood. I placed another sheet over that one and another until the red was no longer visible to the bottlenecking, passers-by. Now, my job was to wait on the coroner to arrive, not by job description, but by instinct. I couldn't leave him there alone on display. I had to stay by his side.

As the hours passed, I must have made thirty calls to the coroner's office to inquire about time-lines. I called so much, they stopped accepting my calls. At the 4-hour mark the coroner van finally arrived, Once again, it was the same young man I had seen in my dreams who had helped me with the suicide. This really startled me, I had only seen him in a dream, and there he was standing before me. We exchanged greetings, and then I hit him with a verbal tirade that would make a drill instructor blush. He tried to explain his whereabouts to me and he had been on scene at a massive auto pile up, but I didn't care. This was an American Airman and he did not deserve to sit out in the 120-degree heat for four hours. After I blasted him, we got down to the business at hand and loaded Bill in the van. The coroner's assistant scurried away as quickly as he could. I started to walk back to my truck and the Chief fell in alongside me. He chuckled and said, "You let him have it, Sarge." I turned to him with contempt in my heart and said, *"Yes I did Chief, yes I did."* I dropped the Chief off at the office and hit the road home. I needed beer in a bad way and I needed to decompress. I wanted to cry, but I couldn't. I could not allow myself to feel the loss of my friend.

When I got home I had a beer in hand before I even got out of my uniform. I drank until I was numb. Several times my wife tried to comfort me but I told her to go away; I couldn't share this pain, it was too raw. I noticed my children were upset; they were scared, too. Their friends had just lost their father. This event made my job real for them. Daddy was the angel of death. My daughter came to me that night and asked me why he died. I told her, *"I wish I fucking knew."* Almost immediately I wanted to take it back and tell her something profound that would make her feel better, but she had already ran to her room in a ball of tears. I had no words. I fell asleep that night and had a dream that would haunt me for years. I was walking from my truck in the parking lot where the accident had occurred. My feet felt like concrete. I could see Crista, lying there limp. And

Bill was under the forklift, screaming. I tried to run to them but I couldn't. The harder I tried the slower I ran. When I made it to the accident site, Crista was gone and the only one left was me and the forklift. I hear a small whimper under the forklift. I kneel down and see Bill. A tear falls from his cheek as he reaches for me, I give him my hand and he says in a low whisper, "Get this fucking thing off me J." I tell him, *"I'm working on it man."* He whispers again, "It hurts! It hurts bad! Please, get this thing off of me!" I let go of his hand and walk away. I know I can't help him. As soon as the forklift is moved he will bleed out. I could not stay there and watch him die. I left a man, no a friend, behind to die alone. I know it's just a dream but I have it a lot. It seems I can't escape it, to this day, if I don't have my service dog with me I freeze in parking lots, paralyzed by fear, hearing those words over and over, *"Get this fucking thing off me J!"*

"IGA Parking Lot" © 2010 Michael Cote, www.flickr.com/photos/cote

The next morning, I was still numb. Not from the beer but from the sheer, emotional toll the case had taken on me. I arrived at base and everyone was talking about what had happened. I walked down the hall and saw the Chaplain that was on scene at the time of the death. She was talking to another officer. I overheard part of her conversation. She said, "It was just a shame. He lived for almost fifteen minutes until they could get that forklift off of him, then he took a breath and that was it." My nightmare was real! I nearly passed out. I had to grab a chair nearby to steady myself. I ran out of the building, got into my truck and went straight home. I didn't ask for permission. I just got in my truck and left.

During the ride home I felt like crying, but I couldn't. It physically hurt to hold it back but something was preventing me from letting it go. When I got home I sat in my chair and stared at the ceiling for hours, unable to process a single thought. They hit me fast, like I was falling from a plane with no parachute. I couldn't focus on anything. I finally fell asleep from exhaustion and when my wife woke me up it was the next morning. I jumped out of the chair and rushed to get ready for work. I was worried that the Commander would be upset with me for leaving the day prior without his consent. When I got to the office the Commander was there waiting for me. He had not realized I was gone the day prior because Crista was still in the hospital and Bill was undergoing his autopsy. He had just stopped by to see how things were progressing. I was relieved to say the least. But now I needed to refocus because I had to plan the family briefing with Crista when she was released from the hospital, an event I was not looking forward to.

A couple of days went by and Crista was released from the hospital. She was staying with friends to aide in her recovery, so we scheduled a briefing with Crista for late on the same day she was released. I knew it would be tough because she had been a First Sergeant and had gone on family notifications and mortuary benefits briefings in the past. I met with the Commander and gave him directions to the house where she was staying. I told him I would meet him there. I left early to change into my dress blues at my own home because the house we were meeting Crista at was very close to my own. I got dressed and nervously paced the floor at my home. I knew this would not be the typical briefing where I would fade into the background and say nothing unless asked directly. I was worried; I couldn't share with her the images I had from the scene that day. I felt as if I was helpless and did not know what to expect but backing out of the briefing was not an option. The only way I can describe how I felt that day is it was like I was standing at the edge of the high dive at a swimming pool, crippled with fear, a line forming behind me. I had to jump and so I did.

I arrived at Crista's friend's house, which was a person I also knew but I cannot recall her name. She met me at the curb and told me that Crista had no recollection of the events; she only knows Bill is dead. I sighed heavily and nodded. I knew she would look to me for answers, answers I did not want to have. But, I prided myself on being 100% honest with the families. I never sugar coated anything. I stepped inside the home and saw Crista sitting inside on a large recliner with her leg in a cast propped up, her body covered in blankets. The Commander moved to her and knelt at her side offering his condolences. She noticed me standing there and looked up at me and said, "Justin, I hoped you would never be standing in my living room giving me this news, but I am glad Bill is in good hands." A tear rolled down her face and she reached up for me signaling an embrace. I moved to her and gave her a hearty hug and just then a tear rolled down my cheek. I was astonished! *"I can't cry! It's not right."* I quickly wiped the tear from my face and stood up.

The Commander stepped in and began his briefing with her. She signed all the paperwork and as we turned to leave she stopped me, "Were you there?" I told her, *"I arrived shortly after he passed. I stayed with him until they came."* She then asked me something that makes me nauseated even as I write this: "Was it quick? Did he die quickly?" Knowing that he struggled for some time and bled out only after the forklift was lifted off of him some fifteen minutes after impact, I was at a crossroads. I thought to myself, *"Do I tell her the truth and cause more pain? Or do I lie and carry this pain?"* I looked down at her, grabbed her hand and said, *"He died on impact; there was no suffering."* She looked relieved, but I wasn't.

I was filling with guilt. Not only had I lied, I had broken a vow I made to myself never to soften the blow even if it made the family feel better. I turned to walk out and Crista stopped me one more time. She asked me to get Bill's phone so she could alert his family. He kept all of his family and friends' numbers on the phone, I agreed and left. As I was walking to the truck, the Commander stopped to assure me that I had done the right thing. He had no problems with me softening the truth for Crista. Still, I did not feel good about doing it. As a matter of fact, I was a little angry with him for not stepping in and correcting the lie. I got in the truck and telephoned the coroner's office. But no one answered. Apparently, I was still blocked from calling them so many times in the previous days. I decided to drive to the location so I could retrieve the phone; I buckled my seat belt and headed into town.

I arrived at the coroner's office about thirty minutes after I had left, and parked the truck. I walked into the reception area, showed my ID and told them my business. The receptionist asked me to wait; they would have someone right out to see me. I was still in my dress blues so I looked rather official which always helped in these situations. After about five minutes an individual who looked to be a doctor came out and asked me to follow him to the back so he could render the personal effects. I followed him down a long hallway, passing room after room with bodies laid open in different stages of the autopsy process. If I hadn't experienced this myself during waking hours I have would have sworn I was having a nightmare. When we arrived at his office, he picked up a gallon sized plastic bag with the name "Bill Biel" written on it in black marker. He handed me the bag, the inventory sheet and requested I sign for the property. I looked over the contents, spotted the phone, a wallet and some jewelry, all covered in blood. I signed the release and headed back to my office. I could not return Bill's phone to Crista in that condition. I had to clean it and ensure it was charged.

I laid down a towel, got some gloves and alcohol wipes out and removed the contents from the bag. I started with the phone. The first thing I noticed was that it was the exact same make and model as my phone. I felt confident I could navigate though it quickly and would be able to charge it on the way back to the house with my car charger. I cleaned it off, key by key. I removed the battery to clean the inside. Blood had dried on the inside of the phone, and it was almost like removing scabs. Once I had finished with the phone I replaced the battery and cleaned the rest of his personal effects. As I was placing the items back into the bag, his phone rang. I did not realize that removing and replacing the battery would cause the phone to turn on. I grabbed the phone and read the caller ID display. It said Mom. I knew I could not answer it. I knew she was mere minutes from getting the worst news of her life and I was the one delivering the device that would strike that blow, and the thought of it turned my stomach. I headed back to the house where Crista was staying and handed over Bill's personal effects. She then asked me to stop by her house and get one of Bills suits. She wanted him buried in his suit because he always found blues to be uncomfortable.

When I walked into her house it was eerily quiet. Pictures of Bill and his family were everywhere. I moved upstairs to where Crista told me the suit would be located and stepped inside his closet. I am now looking through the clothes of a dead man, picking out the last suit he will ever wear. I grabbed the suit and took off to the funeral home to deliver it. As I approached the funeral home I noticed the coroner van out back. I wondered, *"Had he arrived?"* I went inside and met the Funeral Director to give her the suit instructions. The Funeral Director confirmed that Bill's remains had just arrived. I turned away and walked to the prep room. I just left her standing there in mid-sentence. I had to see him. I had to be alone with him.

I approached his remains, all mangled and crushed, but his face was in particularly good shape considering the ordeal he had been through. I leaned over him and whispered, *"What the fuck man? Why?"* I then started to feel so hot and dizzy that I had to hold on to something. I grabbed the table next to me and felt a cold hand. Someone else was on that table. I quickly jerked my hand away and fell to my knees. I sat there for a while trying not to cry but a few tears managed to find their way down my cheeks. Just as I am getting to my feet the Funeral Director walked in and asked if I was all right. I told her, *"He was my friend."* She responded with, "Well, he's in a better place now." I snapped, *"A better place? And where might that be?"* She shot me a puzzled look and I continued, *"Please don't waste your sentimental, he's with the angels bullshit on me!" He is dead! Gone! Finished! And I have to pick up the pieces, while he, is in this better place. Well, fuck your better place!"* I walked out feeling terrible at releasing my anger on her. She did not deserve it; I think I made it almost five minutes before I called her filled with apology and remorse. She understood and told me that grief rears its head in many ways. I was relieved; I hung up the phone and headed home.

That night, I tossed and turned before falling to sleep. There I was again in that parking lot alone and scared. This time I tried to run away but the faster and farther I ran, the closer I got to the forklift. I relived that day several more times that night. The dream kept replaying over and over. I awoke covered in sweat, confused and angry.

Nevertheless, I had to push through this pain. The next several days went by in a blur. Soon it was time to attend the memorial service at the funeral chapel. My son had asked me the day prior if he could attend. At first, I was hesitant to show him my world. But he was hurting so much himself and he wanted to see his friend, so I agreed. We arrived at the chapel where family and friends had congregated on the lawn. I saw Bill's only son standing there all alone, both hands in his pockets. I was going to suggest that Dimitrius go and talk to him. But by the time I opened my mouth to speak he was already half way to him. I watched from afar and saw the smiles they shared. Then in no time at all they were all playing tag. I found this inappropriate at a funeral, but I had never been prouder of my son. He was helping his friend in a way he will never understand.

I went inside and watched family and friends pay their last respects. I asked Dimitrius if he would like to go do the same. He replied, "No dad. He's dead." I just nodded and we left. The next morning I briefed the military escort and began the case paperwork. This event was over and I had made it through. When I think back to this case, I can only sum it up through the words Bill spoke to me in my nightmares, "It hurts. It hurts bad."

CHAPTER 14
And Then I Cried

It had been months since my last case, but I was still struggling with the nightmares and intrusive thoughts. People outside my family were starting to notice that I was struggling. I drove by the mental health clinic more and more often, secretly hoping I would muster the courage to walk in the door and get help. I had developed a good routine of avoiding places that made me remember any of the memories that lurked in my mind. One day, I received a frantic call from my wife. Her mother had had some sort of an attack and was being transported to the hospital via ambulance. I tried to be comforting and tell her everything was going to be fine, but I knew something was wrong. I hung up the phone and called my father-in-law to ask for an update. He told me she appeared to have suffered a heart attack. I asked him to call me with updates; because she wasn't in any condition to hear bad news alone. He agreed and we ended the call.

I need to explain the type of relationship I had with my mother-in-law. In short, we did not get along very well. We were cordial and respectful of each other on most occasions, but I had never liked the way she treated my wife and I wasn't shy about telling her when she stepped over the line. Over the years our relationship grew more and more strained. She and my wife would fight quite a bit. It got to the point that I would tell my mother-in-law when she called that Shar was unavailable, if she had had a particularly bad day. I was also commenting on her idiosyncrasies a lot more, which did not bode well with my mother-in-law. To put it nicely, we did not see eye to eye.

After the news about her mother, Shar had scheduled an appointment to see her doctor. She had recently had a stint of extremely high blood pressure and worried that this event may cause some damage. I told her I wanted to be there with her for the appointment because I was also concerned. I arrived at the clinic at the allotted time and, as I was getting out of my truck my father-in-law called with the news that Shar's mother had passed. She died on the way to the hospital. My heart fell out of my chest, but I knew I was in the right place to deliver the news to my wife. I walked in and Shar was already in the waiting room. I had decided to wait to tell her the news until we were in the presence of her doctor, just in case she needed assistance. We waited for what seemed like hours and were finally ushered into a small exam room. The doctor entered shortly thereafter. He confirmed that her blood pressure was high and he wrote her a prescription for some meds to help control it. At that point, I asked to see the doctor out in the hall. I explained to him what I needed to do. He agreed to be present and we both walked back in the room. I said, *"Shar, I have some bad news."* A scared unsure look fell over her face and her cheeks became flushed. I grabbed her hand and continued, *"Your Mom's gone. She passed on the way to the hospital."* Her hands fell to her side and then we held each other. She did not cry. She put her chin in the air and walked to her car. I was floored. She took it better than I expected. Or did she?

I think sometimes we think we do more harm to ourselves by suppressing our emotions as opposed to allowing ourselves to feel them and move on. My mother-in-law was only 59 years old when she died. I often wish I had made more of an effort to be more tolerant of her. But I know better than most, you can't turn back the clock. My wife and I went home and prepared to tell the kids the bad news. Afterward, we went about the business of planning our trip to San Antonio the next day for the funeral. The kids were crushed. Nanna, as they knew her, always made them smile and was a good grandmother. The next day we drove to San Antonio. I had offered my services in dealing with the funeral home but I was told not to worry, it was handled. I wasn't upset because I had seen it all a hundred times. Sometimes family members choose to get deeply involved in the funeral planning because it keeps the mind occupied and keeps the hurt at bay. Once we arrived I watched the kids and kept them occupied while Shar and her family dealt with the details of the funeral. Oddly enough, this made me feel helpless. I was accustomed to handling everything but I was made to sit this one out.

The funeral was held on base at the same chapel where my wife and I were wed 10 years before. There were flowers, friends and family had gathered to pay their respects. Shar had come from a military family. Her father and brother-in-law were both retired Air Force so we all wore our dress blues to the service. It was your typical service. A picture of my mother-in-law replaced the presence of her remains because she had opted for cremation. A preacher spoke but I did not hear a word he said. My mind had wandered into a far off place. The preacher finished and my brother-in-law got up to say a few words in remembrance of his mother-in-law. The mood was somber and heavy as he spoke. Towards the end of the service the preacher asked if anyone would like to speak. My mind stood still. I felt like I was back in the dream I had had so many times. I tried to stay seated but I could not. My body was on autopilot. My mind raced, my heart pounded. I got to the podium at the front of the chapel. I didn't know what to say. I hear myself telling everyone who I am and what relation I had to the decedent. I tried to stop it. In my mind I screamed as loud as I could, *"STOP!"* Then suddenly the haze lifted and without warning... I cried. Not a normal tear or two, but a deep, profound sob and I couldn't stop. I cried so long and so hard that I couldn't get any words of explanation out. I just stood there and sobbed in front of my wife and children. I sobbed.

I finally mustered the strength to find my seat still weeping. The service ended and we all convened in the parking lot. Nearly everyone in attendance offered me support, saying things like, "You must have really loved her" and "She's in a better place." I nodded still embarrassed at my show of emotion. What no one knew that day was I was not crying for my mother-in-law. I was crying for every man, woman and child I had ever laid to rest. I cried because I couldn't hold it back anymore. I had to release the pain. When I think back to that day, I realize that was the point I finally surrendered and recognized I could no longer walk this path alone. I promised myself in that moment that even if it took the rest of

my life I would seek help. I would overcome this challenge come what may. Until this moment, I was heading down a bad path, drinking too much, ignoring my pain, avoiding the help I really needed, and then... and then I cried.

"Blood Tears" © 2011 Ban Estrada, www.flickr.com/photos/banland/

97

CHAPTER 15
Turning the Page: The Road to Recovery

I decided that day at the funeral I would get help, and the first day I returned to work I went straight to the mental health clinic. I sat in the truck for a while beforehand but I knew what I had to do. Once I mustered up the courage I got out of the truck and went in. It was your typical doctor's office with a waiting area and a reception staff behind a glass wall. I walked up to the glass, pulled out my ID and told the airman I needed an appointment. He told me he would have to check the availability. I stopped him and said, *"Look, it's taken me over a year to get the courage to walk through that door. If I can't be seen today, I will never walk through that door again."* He asked me to have a seat and he would be with me shortly. He had me fill out some paperwork while I was waiting. The forms were tedious and all I could think of was how close I was to getting the help I needed.

After I finished filling in the paperwork, I was greeted by a Hispanic gentleman who told me to follow him to his office. I soon found out he was the counselor that would be working with me. He asked me to have a seat in a large comfortable chair he had in his office. I liked it because I was facing the door and I had grown fond of never having my back to a door. We chatted for a while and he told me his credentials. He asked about my family and where I was originally from. It sounds cheesy but it made me feel at ease. He then asked me what brought me to him. I began to explain my job duties, responsibilities and how I was having nightmares. We spoke for almost two hours discussing all of the things I had seen. He asked me very pointed questions that made me feel like he had been watching me. At the end of this session, I felt relieved that he understood my situation and offered some sense of hope in fixing it. He told me he thought I might have Post Traumatic Stress Disorder or PTSD. He then explained some of the common characteristics associated with the disorder. He set me up with twice a week visits and told me he wanted to do some tests to confirm his initial diagnosis. I left that day with the feeling of a weight being lifted off of my shoulders and a sense of pride that I had the courage to get help.

But I chose not to tell anyone in my squadron. I thought revealing that I had just been diagnosed with PTSD would most certainly end my military career. It was a career killing diagnosis.

I continued to see my therapist and we began doing rapid eye movement therapy. I would follow his finger with my eyes while he moved them rapidly all while retelling my mortuary stories. He explained that the idea behind the therapy is to mimic the mind's processes during REM sleep, which is when the mind categorizes memories. He further explained that the mind has a place for good memories and bad memories. However, the mind doesn't know where to put traumatic memories and that is why they are so easily accessible. This therapy has proven helpful in some patients because it provides them an opportunity to categorize the memories causing them pain. We did this therapy several times. I stopped having the nightmares. I felt safer at work and home but I was still having problems with avoidance.

My therapist suggested that I try getting an assignment in a different line of work. He told me he normally did not suggest avoidance behaviors but since I had seen so much in this one concentrated area that a new base may be just what I needed. I finally went to my Commander and asked to be relived from the mortuary position and was assigned to another area on base performing base exercise planning and working for the Wing Commander. I also started searching out special duty jobs, which are assignments available outside your career path. I found a job available at the Air Force Inspection Agency working on improvement projects for the Air Force. This position was far removed from the mortuary business. I was excited at the chance to apply. I continued to see my doctor and discussed the job with him. He agreed it would be the best thing for my mental health and provide me with the best opportunity to finish my career, no worse for the wear. I applied for the job and was hired within a month. I was walking on clouds. There was finally a light at the end of the tunnel. I could start over at a new base. No one had to know I had PTSD. No one would look at me funny. It was a great day! I finished up my last couple of therapy sessions and was released from doctor's care but he urged me to seek counseling at my new location in New Mexico. I agreed but, in my mind, it was the furthest thing from what I had planned. I was cured!!!! At least, that's what I thought.

A few short months later, I was consumed with the move. We had to secure a home in New Mexico and meet my new co-workers as well as leadership. My initial impression of the base was that it was run down and small compared to the other duty stations I had been assigned to. But, I ended up working at the nicest building on base and had an office that was suited for someone much senior in rank than me. I enjoyed every minute of my new job. I was placed in charge of a new program that monitored the inspection checklist for the entire Air Force. I had arrived!!!!! I was the proverbial big fish now and it wasn't hard to get used to. When I spoke people listened. One email from my office would make entire bases change policies.

A few months after I had arrived, just outside my office window a scene unfolded where a disgruntled boyfriend entered a building and started shooting. I sat there and watched the entire thing. Then I saw the coroners van arrive and they wheeled out the dead bodies. Instantaneously, I was transported in my mind back to that parking lot in Arizona, in the mortuary cooler overseas, holding a man's skull in my hand. I ran out of the building to my truck frozen in fear. My heart rate spiked. I drove home and sat there scared out of my mind. This time it was different. The things I was seeing were much more vivid and painful. My head was pounding. I crawled into bed and sat there weeping. I thought to myself, *"Not this again!"* I wanted to die. I wanted it to stop. My headache grew more intense so I took some over the counter pain relievers and fell into a deep sleep. The next morning I woke up and scheduled an appointment with the local mental health clinic. Once again I told myself, *"This will not beat me."* I was determined to prevail no matter how many times I had to climb this mountain.

I met with my new doctor and discussed my past. He reviewed my records from my previous provider and talked to me about Cognitive Processing Therapy (CPT). This is a form of treatment that focuses on a written recounting of the events that affected me. He gave me very specific instructions and homework to complete. I didn't feel any better and I was on edge. I was determined not to let my PTSD mess up my new job or my career. By chance, I had promised my daughter that I would take her to a large carnival like event on base later that day. I was in no condition to be near large crowds much less walking around inside of one. I picked her up from the day camp she was attending and broke the bad news to her. She was upset and hit me with the one thing more powerful than the PTSD, her tears. I took a deep breath and we went to the fair but I told her we would not stay long. She smiled and started to sing one of her favorite songs.

We arrived at the carnival grounds and started to walk around. Everyone was a suspect. I watched with baited breath waiting for something bad to happen. Just then my daughter shook her hand from mine and said, "Dad, you're hurting my hand. Relax." I must have been gripping her hand too tightly and she always had a knack for telling me like it is. We toured the different food booths, she played the games and it was nearing time to leave. She spotted some of her friends from day camp and asked if she could go see them for a moment. I agreed begrudgingly. Now, I'm standing there alone. To my left, I noticed a booth with a dog next to it. I had three dogs so I decided to go over and check it out. The organization was called Paws and Stripes and the guy running it was talking to another person. I assumed it was a dog rescue so I pulled out a twenty and slipped it in their donation box and then turned to leave. As I walked off, I hear from behind me, "Excuse me?" I turned back around towards the dog booth. It was a young man named Jim Stanek. He reached out his hand and gave me a firm handshake. He told me something that would change my life. He said, "Sarge, if you have any troops that suffer from PTSD, I got the cure, and thank you for your donation." I thought to myself, *"What the fuck ever man."* I immediately regretted my donation and went to find my daughter. I told her it was time to leave.

I stewed over what I had just heard, mocking the young man in my head. *"I got the cure."* The seed, however, was planted. The second I got home I looked up the organization Paws and Stripes on the Internet. I found out they were training shelter dogs to become service animals that recognized the symptoms of PTSD and assisted their handlers by alerting them to oncoming attacks. I had never heard of this. I dug further and found article after article about the benefit of service animals aiding in PTSD. I then tried to dismantle the organization in my mind by searching diligently for something they were doing wrong. I could not find anything; they were legit. I mentioned it to my therapist during our next session and he was very supportive of the idea. He quoted documented research to me, which validated the help that service animals provide to those with PTSD. I thought it may be something I could do when I retire, because there is no way the Air Force would ever allow me to bring a dog to work. I shared that sentiment with my therapist and he responded by saying "It doesn't hurt to ask." This idea intrigued me, but it also meant I would have to let those who worked with me know I had PTSD, a thought I struggled with.

I went back to my office and thought about the possibilities. I knew it would be tough because no one I ever knew had a service dog and the military did not have the best track record for supporting those who were deemed mentally disabled. I decided I would give it a shot and scheduled a meeting with my leadership. I sat in the room surrounded by high-ranking individuals and started to tell my story. I explained to them how a service animal could potentially help me, and the process I would have to go through to ensure the dog is trained correctly for certification. Almost without any discussion my director told me he thought it was a great idea and he would run it up the chain of command. I was floored! They were supporting me.

It took a few weeks to get the proposal run up the chain of command. While I was waiting, I met with the founders of Paws and Stripes and the dog trainers. We mapped out a plan of attack, if approval was granted. Finally, I heard back from the Commander at Headquarters Air Force and they told me to start the training. I had been approved to serve with the aid of a service dog. I also found out I was the first member in the armed forces to be allowed to serve with a service dog. I was ecstatic and called the Paws and Stripes organization to tell them the good news. Paws and Stripes utilized rescue dogs as service animals but I had three dogs already in my home, so I requested an exception to policy to be able to utilize my English Bulldog, Dallas. They agreed, after she passed the trainers' evaluation for service. Six months later she was certified and has been by my side ever since. She is not a cure but she alerts me when things are going to get bad. She can smell the change in brain chemistry and she tells me prior to an attack.

I cannot tell you it has been easy, but having Dallas with me all the time has changed my life. I no longer make excuses nor do I apologize for my PTSD. I embrace it and day-by-day, minute-by-minute, I am getting better. I still have my bad days but they are just that... bad days, they don't control me, nor do they dictate what I do or where I will go.

CONCLUSION

I started this book with a bible verse, so it's befitting that I end it in the same manner. *"Be on your guard; stand firm in the faith; be men of courage; be strong." (Corinthians 16:13)* I am in no way a spiritual man but these words are my savior. They enlighten me, help me to heal, and draw me closer to my fellow man. I have struggled for way too long and I am finally at a point that I am ready to put my fear to the side and walk the path of a man of courage. Will I stumble? Will I fall? Undoubtedly, the answer is yes. But I have the tools and the support to overcome any challenge. The military has been very supportive of me during this entire process and for that I am grateful. But there is more work to do. Everyday a veteran is denied benefits and treated poorly. These men and women gave freely of themselves and should be revered now and forever. Never can we, as a society, repeat the injustices that have happened to veterans returning home from war after Vietnam. Sometimes, as it is in most societies, we treat those we revere the most with the heaviest amount of criticism and hate. I wrote this book to pull the curtain back and offer you a glimpse of how a normal man from a normal town when faced with abnormal circumstances can be affected for a lifetime. If my story touched you in any way, reach out to a veteran. After all, you owe them your freedom.

SPECIAL THANKS

My mother and father, Nancy and David Jordan, my brother, Daron Jordan, Derek Kelly, Matt Harper, Larry Gowen, Erik Shaw, Jeremy Farnes, Paws and Stripes, The BRN Radio Network, the entire Dangerous Conversations team, Scott Ledger, Cynthia Tarana Cone, John Reilly, John Silvagni, Carrie Leyva Gowen, Jeanette Roberts, Brian Southard, Mike Ward, Lyle Haws, Catherine Haws, Susan Isaac Metzler, Ryan Coonfare, Armando Salerno, Armando Salerno, LuAnn Graham, Jean McLaughlin Vanderaar, Charles O'Connors, James Stanek Jr, Lindsey Kay Stanek, Tracy Cook, Kyle Killian, Misty Odell, Jack and Ginia Stiefel, Chelsie Lee, Thomas Connor, Steven Zupic, Jared Chichester, Jennifer Klingman Roberts, Bob Arnold, Jo Pennington, Christopher Starnes, Scott Bullock, Katie Connelly, Nick Capone, Amanda McCoy, Cy Mulholland, R.a. Roman, Christy Faulkner, Jessica Meadows, Christina Nadal, Suzi Toppin, Ilea Anderson, Denise Baker, Randy Hahn, Bill Amell, Nena Stillwell, JoDee Justus, Sarah Diane, Andrea Cooper Wells, John Lane, Mary Beth Pritchett-Lyons, Gigi Ellis, Jessa Bocanegra Walls, Travis Zink, Heidi Graham Bozick, Don McGruder, Joey Hooker, Eric Mayoral, Jason Thacker, Kelly Shane Richardson, James Presley, Carol Ron Marrujo, Patricia Lara, Sonita Johansen, Lyman Woodworth, Karin Westberg Kiltz, Deb Robinson, Keith Petersen, Joe Altieri, Beth Bieren, Donna Harrington, Shannon Edmonds, Scott Bort, Archie LaBrecque, Debbie Brown, Donna White Walle, Adrienne Luster, Brad Yurkovich, Murlene Norris Crowley, Jamie Voelker, Jennifer Lawless Isaacson, Joe Lashley, Dave Barletta, Jennifer Rhodes, Christine Marie Szetela, Ryan Torres, Robert DuBois, Lawrence Ross, Steve Graham, Joe Sears, Dr. Garry Craighead, Willie Rideout, Ashley Emerson, Michael Hammond, Craig Wood, Dawn Erhardt, Michael DuBois, Brandon White, Eric Ramirez

CREDITS

Publishing: Tactical 16, LLC
CEO, Tactical 16: Erik Shaw
President, Tactical 16: Jeremy Farnes
Peer Editors: Christin Barden, Sarah Bowen, Marilyn Pfaff
Cover Design: Kristen Shaw
Cover Photos: *(top)* Photo by Justin Jordan, with model A1C Jeanette Roberts (Now SSgt) / *(bottom)* Photo by Zoriah - www.zoriah.com, www.zoriah.net

All photos/images contained within this publication are used with permission and/or under the appropriate license.

....

PROJECT INVESTORS

Anita Allen

Marcus & Amy Radloff

Jenn Benitez

Bill Bennett

Beth Bozarth

Ben Brown

Lynnette Bukowski

Mary Alice Cloukey

Mike DuBois

Chris Hernandez

Joseph Neri

Charles O`Connors

Chris Olson

Angela Pena

Dawn Piniak

Theresa Presley

Laura Ring

Karen Rokosny

Eleni Roumel

Nena Stillwell

Jessica Sunderland

Jonah Thompson

Mark Trynor

Dennis Tudor

Michael Vick

Tamara Wilson

ABOUT THE PUBLISHER
Tactical 16, LLC

Tactical 16 is a Veteran owned and operated publishing and apparel company based in the beautiful mountain city of Colorado Springs, Colorado. What started as an idea among like-minded people has grown into reality.

What makes Tactical 16 different is our objective to work with Veteran, non-profit organizations by bringing attention to and donating portions of our proceeds through the sales of books and logoed apparel. This is just the start. By buying products from our site or at an event, you will be helping those organizations.

We are a proud supporter of Our Country and its People, without which we would not be able to make Tactical 16 a reality.

How did Tactical 16 get its name? There are two parts to the name, "Tactical" and "16". Each has a different meaning. Tactical refers to the Armed Forces, Police, Fire, and Rescue communities or any group who loves, believes in, and supports Our Country. The "16" is the number of acres of the World Trade Center complex that was destroyed on that harrowing day of September 11, 2001. That day will be forever ingrained in the memories of many generations of Americans. But that day is also a reminder of the resolve of this Country's People and the courage, dedication, honor, and integrity of our Armed Forces, Police, Fire, and Rescue communities. Without Americans willing to risk their lives to defend and protect Our Country, we would not have the opportunities we have before us today.

More works from Tactical 16 available at www.tactical16.com or www.amazon.com.

Brave Rifles

The true story of the trials and tribulations of an American Soldier

By: Erik Shaw

Proof of Our Resolve

By: Chris Hernandez

CPSIA information can be obtained
at www.ICGtesting.com
Printed in the USA
LVOW10*0256090117

520253LV00005B/37/P